Short Introduction to Accounting

An introduction to the fundamentals of accounting and how it is used that will
help students apply accounting as a usable, everyday business tool. It adopts
an intuitive, informal approach to describe basic principles – what they are,
why they exist and how they are used – to help students see the connections
between different parts of accounting and the rest of the business world.
Written by an award-winning teacher, it encourages students to engage with
the material by using questions and worked examples to test knowledge and
understanding as they read. It includes a glossary of financial terms that is a
useful guide to the language of business.

RICHARD BARKER is Senior Lecturer in Accounting at the Judge Business
School, University of Cambridge, and Visiting Professor in Accounting at the
Saïd Business School, University of Oxford.

Cambridge Short Introductions to Management

Series editors: Cary L. Cooper CBE, Lancaster University
Thomas G. Cummings, University of Southern California

The purpose of this innovative series is to provide short, authoritative, reasonably priced books for students taking a first course in Management, particularly at MBA and Master's level. The books include concise coverage of the key concepts taught in the core subjects, as well as suggestions for further study. Written by a team of experts from the world's leading business schools, these books are highly recommended for anyone preparing to study for an advanced management qualification.

For supplementary materials, visit the series website: www.cambridge.org/csi

About the series editors:

Cary L. Cooper is Distinguished Professor of Organizational Psychology and Health, and Pro Vice-Chancellor at Lancaster University. He is the author/editor of over 120 books and is a frequent contributor to national newspapers, TV and radio. Professor Cooper is a past president of the British Academy of Management, a companion of the Chartered Management Institute and one of the first UK-based fellows of the (American) Academy of Management. In 2001, Professor Cooper was awarded a CBE in the Queen's Birthday Honours List for his contribution to occupational safety and health.

Thomas G. Cummings is a leading international scholar and consultant on strategic change and designing high-performance organisations. He is Professor and Chair of the Department of Management and Organization at the Marshall School of Business, University of Southern California. He has authored over 70 articles and 22 books. Professor Cummings was the 61st President of the Academy of Management, the largest professional association of management scholars in the world with a total membership of over 19,000.

Short Introduction to Accounting

Richard Barker

CAMBRIDGE
UNIVERSITY PRESS

CAMBRIDGE UNIVERSITY PRESS
Cambridge, New York, Melbourne, Madrid, Cape Town,
Singapore, São Paulo, Delhi, Tokyo, Mexico City

Cambridge University Press
The Edinburgh Building, Cambridge CB2 8RU, UK

Published in the United States of America by Cambridge University Press, New York

www.cambridge.org
Information on this title: www.cambridge.org/9780521179478

First published 2011

Printed in the United Kingdom at the University Press, Cambridge

A catalogue record for this publication is available from the British Library

Library of Congress Cataloguing in Publication data
Barker, Richard.
  Short introduction to accounting / Richard Barker.
  ISBN 978-1-107-00440-5 (hardback)
  1. Accounting.   I. Title.
  HF5636.B37   2011
  657–dc22
  2011002699

ISBN 978-1-107-00440-5 Hardback
ISBN 978-0-521-17947-8 Paperback

Contents

Figures

Tables

Introduction

Accounting: a subject widely important yet not widely understood

Your choice to read this book is probably determined by a perception that accounting is important, coupled with a sense that your own knowledge of accounting, at least at present, is insufficient for your needs.

In this introductory chapter, we will explore these motivations – in effect, why you are reading this book. This will be important in setting the scene for the rest of the book. The focus will be on you, on why an understanding of accounting is important for you, and on how best you can get your mind around the subject.

We will first explore *why* knowledge of accounting is important. This will help in motivating your study and in contextualising and making sense of the content of this book. We will then explore why accounting is typically perceived to be a difficult and impenetrable subject. This concerns a more subtle motivation for you, namely that you have probably chosen an introductory book because anything else might feel daunting. Such feelings are typical, but actually may not be well placed. Understanding why people typically find accounting difficult, or perhaps more accurately why they perceive it to be difficult, will help greatly in making it simpler and in giving you confidence in your learning.

Before continuing reading, it will be helpful to pause, and for you to ask yourself why you think that accounting is important. Why do you want to learn about it? What do you expect to be able to understand or do, having read this book, that you cannot currently understand or do? Why do you feel that your current knowledge is insufficient for your needs? Are there specific issues that you have in mind, or do you simply feel a general sense that your understanding is not what you would like it to be?

These questions are important. If you have a clear objective in mind in reading this book, and if that objective is reasonable and achievable, then you are in good shape. It will be straightforward to judge whether the book has the content that you need, and whether your expectations are likely to be met. It is more likely, however, that the purpose of learning accounting is not entirely clear. You may believe the accepted wisdom, held among peers and others, that accounting is important, yet it might not be clear why this is so. In what ways, for example, does accounting actually help in understanding business performance and making better decisions? It is important, as we will see, to try to explore these issues more fully. By so doing, we will establish a more powerful foundation for learning.

Why is accounting important?

There is a very simple reason why accounting is important. As a society, we care about wealth, including whether wealth is increasing or decreasing, and whether it is distributed equitably. In order to keep track of wealth, we need a measurement system. Accounting *is* this system.

If we want to know the profit or loss made by an organisation, we refer to its accounts; we are seeking to understand *financial performance*, which is reported in an income statement (otherwise known as a profit and loss account). If we want to know the wealth of an organisation, we also refer to its accounts; our concern here is with *financial position*, which is reported in a balance sheet. Now, there is a lot more to be said about accounting than this, of course, but in essence the importance of accounting is simply that it measures financial activity. It is the measurement system with which we evaluate financial performance and financial position.

This simple conclusion is likely to have several implications for you, and for the value to you in reading this book. These can be summarised as follows.

Financial decision making   Accounting data provide the input to a whole range of decisions, for example the pricing and costing of products and services, the acquisition or divestment of businesses, the evaluation of business plans, and the issue of loans or shares. In order for you to be able to make good use of accounting information in the context of these decisions, it is important for you to understand whether and how that information can be relied upon – i.e. to understand the strengths and weaknesses of accounting as a measurement system. Information that is not understood is apt to be used incorrectly, leading to decisions with adverse economic consequences.

Performance measurement   It is almost certainly the case that the evaluation of your own job performance relies, in one way or another, upon accounting information. You may have responsibility for the profit or loss of a business operation, or for a cost centre, or for the management of assets. Your performance may be measured in financial terms, for example, revenue, expenses, return on capital, or cash flow, and you may be rewarded by means of a financial metric, for example as a percentage of profit or by stock options linked to your company's share price. In all of these cases, it will help you personally to understand how the numbers are put together to evaluate your performance. This is particularly important because, for reasons that we will explore in this book, accounting information is inherently subjective. There is no 'right answer' for the amount of profit that an organisation makes. Rather, there is a range of numbers, any one of which could reasonably and justifiably be called profit. This being the case, and the number that is determined being of great importance to you personally, it matters that profit is not taken as given but that you understand and are engaged in the process by which it is determined.

'Language of business' Accounting terminology is ubiquitous. Management meetings make full and frequent use of the accounting lexicon, referring, for example, to revenue, cash flow, depreciation, capitalising, expensing, provisions, assets, profit, margins, liquidity, return on capital and so on. As with any language, some people can understand what is being said and others cannot. For the latter group, the conversation is awkward and uncomfortable. This is particularly the case because the terms being used are, in some sense, fundamental to the organisation: it is unavoidable, for example, that profit and return on capital are centres of attention. Accounting is therefore not just important but also divisive, in the sense that those 'in the know' are in a position of power, and probably also of career progression, while those unable to speak the language are at an obvious disadvantage. The motivation to learn accounting often comes from this source, in effect from a feeling of insecurity and exclusion. If, through this book, you can get your mind around the role of accounting in economic decision making, and in the assessment of your performance, then confidence in management meetings will follow. And when you get there, you will have transitioned from being silenced by a foreign language to enjoying being able to speak that language.

Why is accounting perceived to be a difficult subject?

Accounting is commonly perceived to be difficult to understand. The reality, however, is that accounting is not rocket science. For example, you do not need to be good at maths to be an accountant, any more than you need to be good at maths to manage your own bank account. Neither do you need some special capacity for understanding, any more than you need special capacity to comprehend how your bank account fits into the overall picture of your personal finances. In short, you probably perceive accounting to be more difficult than it really is.

This is not, of course, to say that accounting is very simple and easily learned. And neither is it to deny that there are challenges in applying accounting knowledge to the real-world complexities of any given organisation, which is often not straightforward, even to the most expert of accountants. It *is* the case, however, that accounting is commonly perceived to be more difficult than it really is. It will help with your confidence in learning accounting to identify and discuss the reasons for this, as follows.

Financial statements are not particularly customer-oriented   In most sectors of the economy, there is a very direct relationship between customers and suppliers. Moreover, competitive forces typically dictate that suppliers owe their economic survival to meeting customer needs, and to doing so with increasing effectiveness over time. Accounting is not quite like that. There exist suppliers of accounting information, namely companies, working with their auditors, and there exist customers also, in the sense that investors and other stakeholders are active users of accounting information. But the process of continuous improvement to meet customer needs is, for the most part, conspicuous by its absence. If you find it difficult to read the accounts in a company's annual report, you are not alone. You may have concluded, correctly, that the accounts are not designed with ease of reading primarily in mind. It is perhaps best to view a set of accounts as the minimum of information that meets regulatory requirements. Companies report what they are required to report, and auditors make sure that regulations are met. Neither the company nor the auditor need ever meet you, the customer, to discuss what information you might require, and in what form; the information is simply not designed in that way. You should not, therefore, be unduly hard upon yourself if you find the accounts difficult to read.

Accountants are preparers, not users   If you train as an accountant, you learn how to create a set of accounts from a mass of individual transactions and events. You learn about accounting standards, tax laws, auditing standards and other relevant regulation and guidance. In short, you become expert in preparing accounts. Once the accounts have been signed off, however, your job is done. Accordingly, you actually learn surprisingly little about what somebody is supposed to do with a set of accounts once it has been prepared. This has two problems. First, it reinforces the lack of customer orientation described above. Second, while non-accountants reasonably assume that accountants know all there is to know about accounting, this turns out to be something of a mistake: accountants are preparers not users, they are taught to build a car but not to drive one. Moreover, the mistake is typically made by accountants themselves. They, too, assume that because they are qualified as accountants, they must be experts in accounting. They can therefore represent themselves as driving instructors. Certainly, they have no incentive to represent themselves otherwise. Most accounting textbooks also reflect this preparer-oriented shortcoming, for example choosing to focus on how to apply accounting standards to produce accounts, rather than on the inherent usefulness of the information that is generated. In general, however, you should not assume that others, including those with accounting expertise, are at much of an advantage to you when it comes to using financial statements. Your reasons to be confident are greater than you probably realise.

Accounts need context   To borrow from John Donne: no set of accounts 'is an island, entire of itself'. There is very limited value in attempting to interpret accounting information without understanding its context. The good news for you is that, for sets of accounts in which you have an interest, for example those of your employer, you may already have the contextual information that you need, meaning that you start at an advantage. So, for example, the issue of how best to measure revenue is a common problem for technology companies. The best solution cannot be reached through an understanding of accounting alone, because it also requires knowledge of the underlying technology and of the company's business model, because these are the things that the accounting is attempting to measure. Likewise, accounting for inventory or for amounts receivable from customers is fairly simple if, but only if, you already have an understanding of the organisation's operations and customers. In short, you should see an understanding of accounting as a natural extension of the knowledge that you already have, and you should seek to understand accounting by means of contextualising it. If, instead, you view accounting as a technical subject, to be studied in isolation, then you put yourself at a disadvantage, because you assume that there is more to the subject than there really is.

This discussion highlights reasons why accounting has the appearance of being difficult. As mentioned earlier, however, this is not to say that accounting is very simple and easily learned. It is also worth exploring these real challenges in learning accounting. Understanding these will help your capacity to learn. These challenges may be grouped under five headings, as follows.

A unique way of thinking   As this book will explain, there is a specific and unique way of thinking that is central to the way that accounting works. This is the so-called 'double-entry' method, which is at the heart of the recording of accounting information and the construction and presentation of financial statements. Getting your mind around the double-entry method is fundamental to an understanding of accounting, but the method may not be intuitive, and it is likely to differ from anything else you will have learned. Once you have grasped the essence of the method, you will see that a great strength of the double-entry accounting model is its inherent simplicity, yet you may need to be patient, as it can take some time and effort to reach the point where this simplicity becomes apparent. This sets accounting apart from many other subjects. Typically, a subject is simple when taken at an introductory level and it becomes increasingly complicated and difficult to understand as the levels are taken higher. Accounting is, in some sense, the opposite. It has a high entry barrier, meaning that a basic understanding of the essentials of the subject can be difficult to achieve, yet once this point is reached, the implicit and enduring simplicity of the double-entry accounting model starts to work in your favour. The good news, therefore, is that this book provides you with a more comprehensive foundation than you might have expected, because you can go a long way having grasped the fundamentals.

All data are connected   Accounting is a measurement system, and each part of that system is in some way related to each other part. This increases the challenge in building your knowledge of the subject because understanding one part of the system requires, to some degree, understanding the other parts also. For example, the method of accounting for an item of machinery requires a simultaneous understanding of how assets are valued, how cash flows are recorded and how profit is measured. At some point, everything will come together, and a subject that may have seemed incredibly complex all of a sudden becomes greatly simplified. So, it will become instinctive and obvious why accounting for the above item of machinery is not just a question of asset valuation, but also of cash flow and profit. But it will take some time and effort to be able to make these connections.

Accounting is subjective   A subject is no doubt easier to understand if there is always a right answer, and if it is always possible to know when that answer has been achieved. Accounting is not quite like that. Assets can be valued in different ways, and a choice between different, equally reasonable assumptions will lead to different determinations of profit. It is important, therefore, to approach the study of accounting with a willingness to accept ambiguity, and to seek to understand the reasons why the ambiguity arises.

Accounting is incomplete   We cannot measure everything, and so the accounts cannot be a complete record of financial performance and financial position. For example, a pharmaceutical company may make a breakthrough discovery, but at the time that this discovery is made, it is not possible to estimate with any reliability how much the discovery will prove to be worth. In other words, while the company undoubtedly has an asset, we are unable to measure that asset's value. It follows that, although it is natural to think of total assets on a company's balance sheet as being a complete measure of wealth, this is not quite accurate because an asset that cannot be valued also cannot be reported on a balance sheet. In order to understand accounting, we must therefore appreciate the limitations of what we are able to measure.

Accounts provide high-level summaries   If you look at the financial statements of a public company, you will not actually find that many numbers. It might be the case, for example, that a single number called revenue aggregates thousands of units of sales of hundreds of different products, each made at different periods of time across multiple markets. Likewise, thousands of transactions, ranging from the employment of people, to the purchase of services, to the consumption of goods, might all be added together into a single number called expenses. It is inevitable that accounting information must be highly aggregated in this way, because it is summarising considerable underlying volume and complexity. It is equally inevitable, therefore, that the majority of an organisation's accounting information is, in effect, unobservable. As a user of accounts, you are looking at a model of reality, built upon a series of assumptions, rather than looking directly at the reality itself, and this abstraction can make it more difficult to know what is going on. If, instead of relying upon high-level summaries, you choose to dig down into the details of the accounting information, then the opposite problem arises, namely that you can become overwhelmed by the sheer volume of data, and by the linkages among each of the components of the overall data set.

These are all good reasons why accounting information can be difficult to understand. In some cases, the issue is simply one of getting your mind around how the double-entry accounting model works, for which this book will help greatly. In some other cases, the problem is more fundamental, for example, when it is inherently difficult to measure financial performance or financial position. In these cases accounting information is inherently insufficient or subjective, and this book will help you to identify when these problems arise. This will also help you to recognise where there are challenges in accounting that are beyond the capacity of even the experts to deal with. In these cases, this book will enable you to take part in a debate around accounting issues, without fear that others have the answer and you do not.

The approach in this book

This Introduction has set the scene for this book, and it remains only to describe to you briefly the style of the book, the way in which it is structured, and the ground that will be covered.

The style of the book, as you will have already detected, is intuitive and informal. It is intuitive in the sense that a spirit of enquiry runs throughout the book. For example, we will not simply describe what an income statement is, but additionally we will explore why we have an income statement in the first place, what purpose it is intended to serve, and what strengths and limitations it has in achieving this purpose. The aim is that you will really come to understand what accounting is all about, which will give you a lasting foundation in the subject. But this will be achieved without getting too heavy or serious, because the style will be informal and designed to engage you. You should find that you are constantly being encouraged to think, and trying to ensure that you are mastering what you are reading. This is achieved in two ways. First, you will be posed questions at various stages in the book, and you will also be asked periodically to stop and reflect. You should take these opportunities as they arise. If you can give thought to a question before subsequently reading the answer, your engagement with the subject and your depth of learning are likely to be significantly enhanced. Second, you will have the opportunity to test your knowledge by means of worked examples throughout the book. Practising what you are learning in this way will help greatly, not least in identifying and filling gaps in your knowledge. It is important to remember that, in accounting, information is connected in various ways, and by working through these connections yourself, by way of numerical examples, you will deepen your understanding.

In terms of coverage, this book will not attempt to touch upon all aspects of accounting, nor will it get drawn into too much detail. The aim is to focus on the fundamentals. We will cover the most important components of any set of financial statements, such as revenue, gross margin, operating profit and so on. This focus on a small number of important items will achieve two things. First, it will prevent complexity from compromising clarity. Second, it will provide vital insight into the fundamental purpose, design, strengths and limitations of the financial statements.

This focus on a small number of key variables does not constrain the scope of the book. Indeed, the book will give you a wide-ranging overview, covering the use of accounting information by managers within organisations, the external communication of accounting information through an organisation's report and accounts, and the use made by investors and others of an organisation's published accounts. The focus on key variables will actually make it easier to maintain this wide scope, because we will be concerned with building a general picture, without risk of being sidetracked into details.

While a focus on key variables will be maintained throughout, you will nevertheless find yourself covering a considerable financial vocabulary as you progress through the book. To help you keep on top of this, and as a basis for consolidating and applying your learning, a full glossary of terms is provided at the back of the book.

It remains simply to outline for you the structure and content of the book. There is a basic distinction made between the foundations of accounting, which are covered in Part I of the book, and the applications of accounting, which are covered in Part II.

Part I

Part I of the book will introduce you to the way that accounting works. We will review the purpose of financial statements, the process by which financial transactions and events are recorded in the accounting system, and the ways in which accounting information is presented. By the end of Part I, you will have a comprehensive overview of the foundations of accounting, as follows.

Chapter 1: A guided tour of the financial statements   Chapter 1 will give you an overview of each of the financial statements, so that you can develop a high-level, introductory feel for how these financial statements can be read and interpreted.

Chapter 2: The need for financial information   The primary financial statements are the balance sheet, income statement (profit and loss account), and cash flow statement. Chapter 2 will build on Chapter 1 by exploring in some depth the need for these statements, how they are related to one another, and what information each of them provides.

Chapter 3: Keeping track of economic activity   Chapter 3 will take you through the nuts and bolts of accounting. Understanding where the numbers come from, and how they are fitted together, will greatly increase your insight into the subject of accounting.

Chapter 4: Summary of the foundations of accounting
To conclude and consolidate Part I of the book, Chapter 4 will test your understanding by means of an extended worked example, through which you will build a set of financial statements from a list of underlying transactions and events.

Part II of the book will cover several applications of accounting, such as how the financial statements can help in understanding how an organisation has grown, how effective its financial performance has been, what inherent risks it has in its financial structure, and how accounting can contribute to financial forecasts, budgets and corporate valuation. These applications of accounting will be introduced in a little more depth after the end of Part I.

1 A guided tour of the financial statements

A guided tour of the financial statements

This chapter will introduce you to the financial statements. The idea at this stage is to give you an overview, and to keep it simple. By the end of this chapter, you will know what you are looking at when confronted with a balance sheet, an income statement, or a cash flow statement. You will understand the basic information that these statements provide, and you will be equipped with some of the key questions that typically arise when reading these statements.

Our approach will be to consider the fictional case of Albert, who has set up a small business, which comprises a single employee making furniture. You will be presented with the financial statements for Albert's business, and we will go through the information that these provide. We will adopt a similar approach in the next chapter, using the fictional case of a consultant called Sarah. In her case, we will adopt a much deeper and more questioning approach, for example exploring the reasons why the financial statements are designed as they are, and the ways in which each of the financial statements links with one another. In Albert's case, however, we will keep it simple. This will be a helpful foundation. At later stages in the book, when the content becomes broader and deeper, you might like to refer back to Albert. If you can read and understand the financial statements for his business, and if you know the right questions to ask, then that is a great starting point. Everything else in the book is really just building on this foundation.

Cash flow statement

When Albert started his business, he invested €20,000 (€20k) of his own money and he borrowed €15k from the bank. In his first day of business he used most of this money (€30k) to buy the equipment that is needed to make furniture. Occupying a rented workshop, his

Table 1.1 Albert's cash flow statement for the past financial year

	€k
Cash flow from operating activities	10
Cash flow from investing activities	–30
Cash flow from financing activities	35
Change in cash	15
Opening cash balance	0
Closing cash balance	15

business makes furniture in response to direct demand from his customers. In his first year of business, Albert's cash flow statement was as shown in Table 1.1.

The cash flow statement is perhaps the simplest of the financial statements to understand, because it is just a summary of amounts paid and received in cash during a period of time, rather like a bank statement.

The basic structure of the cash flow statement is the separate categorisation of operating, investing and financing activities. The bottom line of the cash flow statement is the organisation's closing cash balance, just as a bank statement ends with the closing account balance. In Albert's case, the business was started this year, and so the opening cash balance is zero. The overall change in the cash balance during the year is €15k made up of €10k generated by operating activities, €30k invested in equipment and €35k raised in finance to start the business.

Operating cash flows result from trading activities, for example cash received from customers, or cash paid to suppliers or employees. A positive overall operating cash flow, such as that achieved by Albert, is a good sign, because it means that the cash received from customers exceeds the cash paid out to operate the business.

Investing cash flows arise when long-term assets are bought or sold. The purchase of land, buildings or equipment is an investing cash flow. A negative investing cash flow therefore implies growth in the operating capacity of the business. This is the case for Albert: he has spent cash to acquire new equipment. A positive investing cash flow, in contrast, would mean divestment of assets, and a corresponding shrinkage in the business. Unlike operating cash flow, where a positive number can be seen as good news, the interpretation of investing cash flow is ambiguous: a negative number is good news if the corresponding investment is a wise one, while a positive number could also be good news if, for example, assets are disposed of at an attractive price. While investing cash flow does give you an indication of growth or shrinkage in the operating capacity of the business, it cannot indicate whether the investment decisions are good ones.

Financing cash flows arise when the organisation transacts with its providers of long-term finance, for example when cash is received from the issue of new shares, or when cash is paid out to redeem a bank loan. As with investing cash flows, the sign of the flow cannot be interpreted unambiguously. A positive financing cash flow simply means that new finance has been raised, while a negative number means repayment of finance. If, for example, a bank loan is taken out in order to fund a profitable new venture, then a positive financing cash flow can be viewed in a positive light. But the cash flow statement cannot provide this information. It records whether there has been borrowing or lending, but it cannot indicate whether these financing decisions are good ones.

The categories in the cash flow statement are related to one another. For example, if a business wishes to grow its operating capacity, meaning that investing cash flows are negative, then this can be achieved in one of three ways. First, the growth can be achieved organically by reinvesting positive operating cash flow. Second, the organisation can borrow, resulting in a positive financing cash flow. Finally, the organisation can use any existing cash balances that it has at the beginning of the reporting period, in which case the negative investing cash flow is matched by a negative change in cash on the bottom line of the cash flow statement. In Albert's case, €10k is generated organically through operations and €35k is raised through financing. The operating capacity of the business grows by means of a €30k investment in equipment, leaving a closing balance of €15k.

Imagine that you are asked to comment on a company's cash flow statement. The outline above suggests that you might ask questions such as the following.

1. Is the company generating positive operating cash flow?
2. Are investing cash flows negative, meaning that the company is growing? If so, how is this growth being funded?
3. Is the company borrowing, and if so, is the effect to cover negative operating cash flow, to enable investment, or simply to increase the company's bank balance?

An income statement has a very simple purpose, namely to record whether an organisation has made a profit or a loss (hence the statement is often called a 'profit and loss account'). Similar to the cash flow statement, an income statement is a summary for a period of time, such as a year. Albert's income statement for the first year of his business was as shown in Table 1.2.

Our first conclusion from reading Albert's income statement comes from looking at the bottom line. Albert has made a profit of €7k during the current financial year.

The concept of making a profit is very straightforward. It means that the income generated by an organisation exceeds the expenses incurred by that organisation. Equally, of course, if expenses are greater than income, the organisation makes a loss. In general, income less expenses equals profit or loss.

Profit is earned over a period of time. In Albert's case, the profit of €7k is earned over the course of a year. For internal purposes, a company might report its profit on a monthly basis, while it might report to its shareholders quarterly, every six months or annually. The period of time to which the income statement relates is called the reporting period, and profit is always stated with respect to the reporting period during which it was earned.

We do not know whether the performance of Albert's business this year is likely to be typical of his future performance, or instead whether it is likely to prove unusually good or unusually bad. So, while we can conclude that Albert's business is profitable in the current year, we cannot say whether this is representative. We also do not know, of course, whether Albert is more or less profitable than his competitors. For this, we will need to see *their* income statements. In general, therefore, an income statement for a single period is of limited use, and more comprehensive information might be sought by considering other periods of time as well as the financial statements of competitors.

There is more to the income statement, of course, than the bottom line. The other lines in the statement are either revenue, expenses or subtotals. The first line is revenue. The expenses, in Albert's case, are cost of goods sold, salary, rent, depreciation, other operating expenses, interest and tax. The subtotals are gross profit, operating profit and profit before tax. The reason for the separate reporting of revenue, expenses and subtotals is that each of them provides

Table 1.2 Albert's income statement for the past financial year

	€k
Revenue	75
Cost of goods sold	–10
Gross profit	**65**
Salary	–35
Rent	–14
Depreciation	–3
Other operating expenses	–2
Operating profit	**11**
Interest expense	–1
Profit before tax	**10**
Tax	–3
Profit after tax	**7**

different information to the reader of Albert's income statement, as we can see by considering each item in turn.

Revenue (sometimes called turnover, or simply sales) is the value of services provided and/or goods sold during a period of time. This is the volume of output that is achieved multiplied by the price that is charged. It is the amount of money that has been earned during the period by transacting with customers.

This concept of money 'earned' differs in a subtle but important way from money actually received. For example, there might be occasions when Albert makes a sale in one reporting period, but does not collect the cash from his customer until the next period – the sale might have been made on 28 December, but cash settlement is not received until 3 January. On such occasions, revenue for the reporting period includes the value of the sale made during the period even though there is no actual payment but instead a customer's commitment to pay. The basic idea is to measure the value of the output that Albert generates during the period. This is an important theme, and we will return to it in Chapter 2.

Cost of goods sold (sometimes called cost of sales) comprise expenses that are directly attributable to units of output. In Albert's case, and to keep the example simple, we have assumed that the cost of goods sold comprises the materials that go into making his furniture. For each item that he sells, there is a corresponding cost of materials.

Gross profit (sometimes expressed as a percentage gross margin) is a subtotal in the income statement, equal to revenue less cost of goods sold. The gross profit from making a sale is the net benefit to Albert, being the amount that he earns in revenue less the associated costs of goods sold that he has to incur.

The concept of gross profit is sometimes expressed as a percentage gross margin. This is gross profit as a percentage of revenue. In Albert's case, it is 65/75, or 87 per cent. This is a high gross margin, which means that there is a high net benefit to his business from each sale that he makes.

Operating expenses include all of the costs of making and selling furniture, excluding those already charged as costs of goods sold. Very approximately, these costs can be viewed as fixed, as opposed to variable. In other words, they remain broadly the same in any given period of time regardless of the output achieved during that period. In Albert's case, even if he fails to make a single sale, he is likely to continue to pay his employee a salary, he will still be obliged to pay rent on his workshop and his equipment will probably depreciate at a similar rate.

In the same sense that revenue can be earned during a period without cash necessarily being received in that period, so it is also possible for expenses to be incurred even if there is no concurrent cash payment. This is best illustrated in Albert's case with the example of depreciation, which is a measure of how much the value of his equipment has declined in the period, as a result of usage and the passage of time. This decline in value does not involve Albert spending any money. Rather, it involves the loss in value of an asset that Albert already owns. In effect, he is partially consuming an asset that he has to own and operate in order to be able to make furniture. For him, it is a cost of doing business, much like paying rent on his workshop. Both the depreciation and the rent are expenses, yet only the rent is actually a cash payment in the current period. In short, expense and expenditure are not the same thing. An expense is a loss of value during the reporting period, whether this involves spending money (expenditure) or consuming assets (in Albert's case, depreciation on his equipment).

Operating profit is a measure of the gain that Albert achieves by making and selling furniture. This gain will be split three ways. First, Albert will pay interest on the money that he has borrowed from the bank. Second, he will pay tax. Third, the remainder of the profit he will keep for himself. Operating profit is an important subtotal because it measures the total gain made by operating a business, in this case in the furniture industry, out of which distributions can be made to providers of finance and to the government.

Interest expense is the cost of borrowing money from the bank. Albert initially borrowed money from the bank in order to invest in equipment and other assets. This investment generated an operating profit, and now some of that profit must be allocated to paying the cost of borrowing.

Profit before tax is the surplus of operating profit over interest expense. It is the basis on which the organisation's tax liability can be calculated.

Tax, in its simplest form, is calculated as a percentage of profit before tax. In Albert's case the tax rate is 30 per cent.

Profit after tax (sometimes called net income) is the 'bottom line'. It is the amount made by the owners of the business during the reporting period, because it is equal to the total value of the output of the business, less the total of expenses (including interest and tax) incurred to generate that output.

The income statement is the most commonly used and important of the financial statements. It is helpful, therefore, for you to know how to respond if asked to comment on an income statement, for which you will probably be given information from more than just the current year. The outline above suggests that you might ask questions such as the following.

1. Are revenues increasing over time? Is the change due to a greater or smaller volume of output, or to a higher or lower price, or to some combination of the two?
2. Is this a business with a high or a low gross margin? Is the gross margin increasing or decreasing over time? Is the change in the margin due to sales price or to the cost per unit of goods sold? Or is the margin change the result of a change in product mix, whereby products with different margins are now being sold in different relative quantities?
3. Are operating expenses increasing over time, and is the rate of increase faster or slower than that of revenue?
4. Are borrowing expenses increasing over time, and is the interest cost a greater or lesser percentage of operating profit?
5. Is the tax rate changing over time?
6. Is the company profitable, and is it likely to remain so?

As described earlier, Albert started his business with some of his own money, while also borrowing from the bank. He invested in the purchase of equipment. From the outset, therefore, Albert had both assets and liabilities. Specifically, as shown in Table 1.3, he had assets in the form of equipment and cash, and he had a liability in the form of an outstanding bank loan.

The basic structure of the balance sheet is that it comprises assets, liabilities and equity. Assets are items of value that belong to the business. Liabilities are obligations of the business to make payments to third parties. The excess of the assets in the business over its liabilities is called equity. This is the owners' stake in the business. It is sometimes referred to as shareholders' funds. This can be summarised as follows.

Equity = assets – liabilities

or, more concisely,

Equity = net assets

As the balance sheet records the value of the assets and liabilities in a business, it is a statement of financial position. It can be viewed as a summary of the wealth that is tied up in the business. In contrast with the income statement, which records the amount of profit earned during a period of time, the balance sheet exists at a point in time, and it records the financial position at that point. The balance sheet is analogous to the amount held in your bank account at any point in time, while the income statement is analagous to the interest that is earned on your account during a period of time.

A balance sheet is always prepared for both the start and the end of the reporting period covered by an income statement; these are referred to as the opening and closing balance sheets, respectively. In Albert's case, the closing balance sheet in Table 1.4 states his financial position at the end of the period covered by the cash flow and income statements in Tables 1.1 and 1.2.

The assets on a balance sheet are split into two categories: fixed and current. Fixed assets are those that represent the infrastructure of the business. They are held for the long term. They are employed in the business to generate revenue over several reporting periods. In Albert's case, his equipment is a fixed asset. If he owned the

Table 1.3 Albert's balance sheet on his first day of business

		€k
Fixed assets	Equipment	30
Current assets	Cash	5
Total assets		**35**
Long-term liabilities	Bank loan	15
Total liabilities		**15**
Equity		**20**

Table 1.4 Albert's balance sheet at the end of the financial year

		€k
Fixed assets	Equipment	27
Current assets	Inventory	4
	Accounts receivable	6
	Cash	15
Total assets		**52**
Long-term liabilities	Bank loan	15
Current liabilities	Tax payable	3
	Accounts payable	7
Total liabilities		**25**
Equity		**27**

workshop, rather than renting it, then that would also be a fixed asset, as would a delivery van or a sales office.

Current assets, in contrast, are held for the short term, which is typically defined to be less than one year. Current assets can be viewed as part of the organisation's trading cycle. Albert's inventory is a good example. Raw materials are purchased, converted into finished goods, and then sold, to be replaced by a new acquisition of raw materials. Raw materials and finished goods are both acquired and disposed of as part of the organisation's trading cycle, which is typically very much shorter than one year, and inventory is therefore a current asset.

Another current asset is accounts receivable (otherwise known as trade debtors). These are amounts owed by customers to whom Albert has made a sale, but from whom cash has yet to be received.

There is also a one-year distinction made for liabilities on the balance sheet. If the liability is expected to be paid more than a year after the balance sheet date, then it is classified differently from amounts payable within the year. Albert's bank loan, which is not short-term, is therefore classified separately from his tax payable and his accounts payable, both of which will be settled within the year. Accounts payable are, in effect, the opposite of accounts receivable. They are amounts owed to suppliers. In Albert's case, he may have received delivery of raw materials but he has not paid for them.

If you look at the assets on Albert's balance sheet, you will find that they are listed in order of liquidity, meaning nearness to cash. Albert does not intend to sell his equipment: this is not an asset that he wishes to liquidate. Moreover, even if he did decide to sell, he might not be able to do so very quickly, because there may not be a very good second-hand market for woodworking equipment. It might also be the case that he could not get as much for his equipment as he thought it was worth. The nearness to cash of his equipment is therefore remote, and so we would describe this asset as illiquid, while other assets on Albert's balance sheet are relatively liquid, and increasingly so as one progresses down the balance sheet to the final item, cash. The liabilities side of a balance sheet is also ordered in terms of liquidity. So, for example, a bank overdraft is highly liquid because it is repayable on demand, while a long-term bank loan is illiquid, because it is not repayable for several years. In Albert's case, the loan is less liquid than tax payable or accounts payable.

Liquidity is important for two reasons. First, an organisation needs to have sufficiently liquid assets in order that it can meet its obligations as they fall due. Second, greater liquidity implies greater flexibility. If an organisation has committed all of its resources to highly illiquid assets, then it is ill-equipped to cope with an adverse change in economic conditions. For example, if the assets in question are dedicated to the production of a specific type of product, and if the market for that product collapses, then the company is neither able to make money by selling the product, nor able to recover the cash that has been invested in the illiquid asset. If, in contrast, a company has a highly liquid balance sheet, then its resources can be quickly and painlessly diverted from one use to another.

A final comment on liquidity, and on the balance sheet in general, is that there exist different conventions for the presentation of balance sheet information. While assets become more liquid as you read down the balance sheet in Table 1.4, the opposite can also hold, and you will find that some companies report their balance sheet items in the reverse order. Similarly, while Table 1.4 reports in a vertical format, with assets above liabilities, which are in turn above equity, a horizontal format is also common, for example with assets on one side and with liabilities and equity on the other. Different subtotals are also common in practice. You should be aware of this variation in practice, but you need not be concerned about it. The information is the same, and the interpretation of that information is the same also; it is simply that the information can be presented in different ways.

Imagine that you are asked to comment on a company's balance sheet. The outline above suggests that you might ask questions such as the following.

1. Is the business capital-intensive, meaning that it has a relatively high percentage of fixed assets, or does the business have predominantly current assets?
2. How liquid is the balance sheet, for both assets and liabilities?
3. How much of the long-term funding of the business comes from owners/shareholders and how much is from the bank?

Worked example: retail company

It will be helpful at this stage for you to have a go at reading a set of financial statements. Take a look at the income statements, cash flow statements and balance sheets presented in Table 1.5. See what you think. Before reading any further, you should reach your own conclusions about what can be learned about this company from its financial statements. You should also come up with a list of questions, which are prompted by the financial statements, but which those statements alone cannot answer. When you return to the text below, you will see some suggestions on both conclusions that can be reached and on questions that might be asked. This list is not definitive, and you may well come up with valuable ideas beyond those below.

Here are some suggested conclusions about what can be learned about the company by reading its financial statements.

- The business has been growing. Total assets have increased, including fixed assets in the form of stores, inventory located in those stores and accounts receivable generated by sales made in those stores. Revenue increased by nearly €100m over the course of two years.

Table 1.5 Retail company

Income statements (€m)

		Year 1	Year 2	Year 3
Revenue		500	550	595
Cost of goods sold		−425	−468	−506
Gross profit		**75**	**83**	**89**
Salary		−45	−47	−50
Depreciation		−5	−6	−6
Other		−10	−10	−10
Operating profit		**15**	**20**	**23**
Interest expense		−2	−2	−2
Profit before tax		**13**	**18**	**21**
Tax		−4	−5	−6
Profit after tax		**9**	**13**	**15**

Cash flow statements (€m)

Operating cash flow		14	22	24
Investing cash flow		−10	−10	−10
Financing cash flow		−1	−4	−7
Change in cash		**3**	**8**	**7**

Balance sheets (€m)

Fixed assets	Retail stores	55	60	64
Current assets	Inventory	35	39	42
	Accounts receivable	10	11	11
	Cash	28	36	43
Total assets		**128**	**145**	**161**
Long-term liabilities	Bank loan	40	40	40
Current liabilities	Tax payable	4	5	6
	Accounts payable	71	78	84
Total liabilities		**115**	**123**	**131**
Equity		**13**	**22**	**30**

- The business is profitable, and profit after tax has increased as the business has grown. Margins are quite tight, however, with a profit after tax of only 1.8 per cent of revenue in the first year, rising to 2.5 per cent in the third year.

- There is a 15 per cent gross margin, meaning that the costs of goods sold are high on each sale that is made. A small change in the gross margin would have a large impact on the bottom line.
- Operating expenses are increasing somewhat over time, in particular salary. This reduces the beneficial impact of growth on bottom-line profit.
- The business is consistently generating positive operating cash flow.
- The growth of the business is funded by the reinvestment of operating cash flow, and there has been no need to seek additional bank loans or to raise further funds from shareholders. Indeed, it has actually been possible to pay a dividend to shareholders (this is the financing cash flow), while also increasing the amount of cash held by the company.

Here are some suggested questions prompted by the financial statements. For each of these questions, you should note the importance of understanding the business. You will recall that the accounts provide only limited information and they cannot be understood out of context. While accounting information can prompt questions about the business, such as those below, your experience and knowledge of the business will ultimately provide the answers to those questions.

1. How much of the growth in revenue is due to greater volume and how much to higher prices?
2. Gross margins have remained constant, at 15 per cent in each year. Are they expected to remain so, or are there pressures that will cause them to rise or fall?
3. Is the profitability of new stores better or worse than that of existing stores? Is there scope for further profitable expansion?
4. Revenue and gross profit have grown by 18 per cent over two years, while salaries have increased by only 11 per cent and other expenses have remained constant. The result is that profit after tax has increased by 67 per cent. Is this sustainable? In particular, should the business expect there to continue to be relatively low growth in operating expenses?
5. Is there any reason to be concerned about liquidity? In particular, are their circumstances under which obligations to trade suppliers might not be met?
6. Why is the business holding so much cash? The balance sheet for the final year suggests that the bank loan could be repaid in full, thereby reducing interest expenses.

In summary

We have now completed a brief tour of the financial statements. You will find that the basic structure discussed above is used universally. There is considerable variation in presentation, but the essentials are the same. You should now feel able to pick up the financial statements of any organisation and feel that you at least have a starting point. You should know that the income statement reports income, expenses and profit or loss, that the balance sheet reports assets, liabilities and equity, and that the cash flow statement reports operating, investing and financing cash flows. And you should have some sense of what each of these categories means, as well as having in mind a basic set of questions to ask of any organisation's financial statements.

We now have a foundation on which to build. Subsequent chapters in Part I will expand on this by exploring fundamental concepts behind the design of the financial statements, strengths and limitations in accounting information, linkages among the financial statements, and the mechanisms by which financial transactions and events are captured and reported in an accounting system.

2 The need for financial information

Chapter 1 has given you an overview of the information contained in a set of accounts. This chapter will significantly deepen your understanding by means of exploring the underlying logic of accounting. Our approach will be intuitive, asking basic questions and developing simple worked examples. In this way, we will gradually build up an understanding of why we have cash flow statements, income statements and balance sheets in the first place, how and why these statements are related to one another, and what their inherent strengths and weaknesses are.

A first insight is provided by the meaning of the term accounting itself. In general, of course, an account is a story of something that has happened. A financial account is one such story, and its importance comes from its telling of economic activity. If we want to understand the economics of an organisation, then we read its accounts. Whether we are trying to understand how much money the organisation is making, how much it is investing and growing, or how financially secure it is, our starting point is the accounts.

As we have seen in Chapter 1, there are different accounts for different purposes. So, for example, if we want to understand the value of the assets that an organisation controls, then we look to the balance sheet. Alternatively, if our interest is in whether the organisation has managed to increase the value of its assets over time, in other words whether it has become better off, then we look to the income statement.

In general, accounting can be described as a system of measurement. There are three elements to this system: recognition, measurement and presentation.

First, we must identify what to include in the financial statements. For example, while certain assets might belong to an organisation, others might not, and we need to decide which are which. If an item is included in the financial statements, then it is said to be recognised, and the act of inclusion is called recognition. The basic principle of recognition is that we should include an asset in an organisation's accounts only if that organisation has exclusive control over the asset. So, for example, while a road haulage company makes extensive use of the road network, and could not make profits in the absence of this network, it does not own the roads and so they are not recorded as assets in the company's accounts.

Second, we must actually measure the items included in the accounts, which means attributing an economic value to them. For our road haulage company, this means, for example, estimating what its fleet of trucks is worth. There are many disparate transactions and events that are captured in a set of financial statements, and they all have in common that they are measured in monetary terms.

Third, we must present our information in a way that is intelligible to users of the accounts. So, for example, our company's trucks would be presented alongside information relating to other fixed assets and, more broadly, as part of the company's balance sheet.

It is helpful to keep in mind that, in all cases, the method of accounting for any transaction or event comprises the steps just described: identifying what to include in the accounts (recognition), measuring the value of those items (measurement), and then presenting the resulting values in an informative way (presentation).

In order to understand how, in practice, the disparate economic information relating to an organisation is pulled together into a coherent set of financial statements, our approach will be to build these statements from scratch. We will adopt an intuitive approach, exploring at each stage what purpose the accounting is intended to serve. In order to increase the intuitive appeal of the exercise, we will not create the accounts for a commercial organisation, but instead for an individual person. Her name is Sarah. The logic and structure behind accounting for Sarah's economic activity is exactly the same as it would be for a small company, a large multinational or indeed even for a country or for the global economy: the method of accounting is universal. Yet by starting with Sarah, we can keep the example simple, thereby enabling the underlying logic and structure of accounting to be illustrated more clearly, as well as ensuring that the activities we are accounting for are familiar to any one of us.

Remembering that accounting is a system for measuring economic activity, our primary aim in providing accounts for Sarah is to answer some basic economic questions, such as the following.

- How wealthy is Sarah?
- Does Sarah have debts and is she able to pay them?
- Was Sarah's income greater than her expenditure over the course of the past year?
- Can Sarah afford to maintain her current level of spending?

The following discussion will seek to demonstrate how accounting can provide answers to these questions.

Does a bank statement capture economic activity?

Our starting point in analysing Sarah's economic activity will be the simplest and most common form of financial account – something that we all have and use, and for most of us our only financial statement. This is her bank statement, which is presented in Table 2.1. To keep the example simple, we can make the assumption (albeit unrealistic) that Table 2.1 includes all of her bank transactions over the course of the past year.

Our starting point is to consider whether Sarah's bank statement provides answers to the four questions raised above. In other words, if the bank statement is the only financial statement that she has, does she have sufficient information regarding her financial performance and financial position? As we will discover, the answer is that she does not. We will explore the reasons why this is the case, and by so doing we will derive the need for an income statement and a balance sheet as statements that provide supplementary information.

So, take a look at Sarah's bank statement. Consider the four questions that were raised above, and then consider the extent to which the information in the bank statement is able to provide an answer to these questions. In particular, and before continuing to read the next paragraph, try to identify what the intrinsic limitations of the bank statement are. In other words, why is it, in principle, that a bank statement is less than ideal as a summary of economic activity? Try thinking about your own economic activity: why can you not rely on your bank statement alone to answer, for yourself, the four questions raised above?

The intrinsic limitations of the bank statement can be subdivided into two categories: presentational and fundamental. Presentational limitations are straightforward to resolve. They arise simply because the information contained within Sarah's bank statement is not presented in the most useful way. We can therefore resolve

Table 2.1 Sarah's bank statement

	€
Opening balance	8,500.00
Supermarket	−32.70
Cinema	−12.00
Restaurant	−28.65
New car	−8,600.00
Mortgage interest payment	−500.00
Mortgage capital payment	−1,000.00
Supermarket	−94.10
Coffee shop	−8.21
Car insurance	−242.00
Consulting income	5,700.00
Tax on consulting income	−2,280.00
Interest expense	−2.50
Train fare	−18.00
Petrol	−10.00
Coffee shop	−3.59
Supermarket	−14.24
Train fare	−23.90
Petrol	−41.75
Cash withdrawal	−200.00
Supermarket	−9.99
Coffee shop	−6.58
Supermarket	−36.99
Music store	−14.99
Health club	−40.00
Coffee shop	−8.50
Restaurant	−42.36
Closing balance	928.95

the presentational limitations simply by adopting an appropriate categorisation and formatting of the information. In contrast, the fundamental limitations of the bank statement as a source of information cannot be resolved. It becomes necessary to seek additional information. Specifically, and as we shall see, it becomes necessary to create an income statement and a balance sheet.

We will start with the presentational limitations, which are twofold. First, some simple aggregations and rearranging of data make the bank statement more intelligible. It is not helpful, for example, that there are several line items that are described in the same way. While we are likely to want to know how much, in total, Sarah spends on such things as the supermarket or the coffee shop, we are unlikely to be interested in the number of transactions at each place and the value of each individual transaction. Indeed, a proliferation of individual transactional data simply makes an account difficult to read. Similarly, we are likely to find it helpful to separate cash inflows from cash outflows. If we apply simple presentational changes such as these, it becomes much more straightforward to understand where Sarah is generating her cash and what she is spending it on.

The second presentational limitation is perhaps not so obvious, although it is of considerable importance. Sarah's cash flows are of two types, which differ significantly for the purposes of understanding Sarah's economic activity. The critical distinction is that the first type of cash flow changes Sarah's overall wealth, while the second does not. When Sarah buys a cup of coffee, she becomes worse off; she has consumed some of her wealth. In contrast, when she buys an asset, such as a car, she does not become worse off. Rather, she has exchanged an amount of her asset of cash for a different asset valued at the same amount; her cash may have reduced, but her overall wealth stays the same. Similarly, if she pays off part of her mortgage, the amount of cash that she owns is reduced, but so too is the amount that she owes to the bank. And conversely, her bank balance would be increased significantly if she took out a new mortgage, but the increase would be exactly offset by a new amount now owing to the bank, and overall she would be neither better off nor worse off.

Although a bank statement makes allowance for neither of the presentational limitations just described, the typical cash flow statement reported by an organisation addresses both.

The cash flow statement

Table 2.2 illustrates what Sarah's cash flow statement might look like. Several observations can be made about this statement.

As mentioned in Chapter 1, the cash flow statement is very similar to a bank statement, and so in essence it is something that we are all familiar with. It records the opening bank balance, movements in and out of the bank, and the closing bank balance.

Table 2.2 Sarah's cash flow statement

			€	€
Operating cash flow	Inflow		5,700	
	Outflow	Consumables	−415	
		Travel	−336	
		Leisure	−138	
		Interest	−503	
		Income tax	−2,280	**2,029**
Investing cash flow				**−8,600**
Financing cash flow				**−1,000**
Change in cash				**−7,571**
Opening balance				**8,500**
Closing balance				**929**

There are, however, two key differences between a cash flow statement and a bank statement, as follows.

First, while in practice a bank statement is simply a list of all transactions through the bank account, the cash flow statement differs because individual transactions are aggregated to a summary level. Consider, for example, Sarah's spending at the coffee shop. While we could see from our individual transactions exactly how much she had spent at each visit to the coffee shop, this information is no longer transparent in the cash flow statement because it has been aggregated together with other items. Indeed, it is not even obvious which line item includes the coffee shop spending. If Sarah regards coffee shop spending as a necessary part of her routine, then it is likely to be included under the heading of consumables. On the other hand, if it represents a social activity, then it may be shown under the leisure heading. It might even be the case that the coffee shop is located at the train station and that Sarah only goes there when she takes the train, in which case her cash outflow might be reported under the travel heading. The point is that when data are aggregated into summary form, there is some loss of information. We simply cannot be sure, by looking at the cash flow statement alone, where different items have been reported. Moreover, classification can be a matter of subjective opinion, rather than of right or wrong. If we were to compare Sarah's cash flow statement with that of a friend of hers, we may find that each person had taken different classification decisions, for example with coffee reported as a consumable by Sarah but as leisure by her friend. In general, even if a given line in the financial statements is described in the same way in different sets of accounts, the items included need not be directly comparable.

Second, we have introduced three high-level categories of information in the cash flow statement, namely, operating, investing and financing. Each of these categories is intended to provide different types of information. A key distinction can be made between, on the one hand, operating cash flows and, on the other hand, investing and financing cash flows. In essence, operating cash flows are those that change wealth, while investing and financing cash flows are those that do not change wealth. We will return to this key distinction shortly, but first it will be helpful to review, in the context of Sarah's cash flows, the definitions of the operating, investing and financing cash flow categories that were introduced in Chapter 1.

Operating cash flows are typically concerned with regular activities. For Sarah, this covers the consulting income that she receives each month, and her regular cash outflows, which include taxation, and spending at the supermarket, the coffee shop, the train station and so on. For a company, operating cash flows would include revenue from sales, payments for materials and other goods and services received, payment of employees and so on.

In contrast, investing cash flows are the outcome of investment decisions. For Sarah, the purchase of a house or a car is an investment decision because she is acquiring an asset that will serve her for several years, and that she is likely to be able to sell once she has finished using it. Cash outflow occurs when the investment is made and cash inflow occurs at a later date when the acquired asset is sold. For a company, investing cash flows would include the acquisition or disposal of land, buildings or plant and equipment, as well as the acquisition or disposal of entire businesses. Hence, investing cash flows involve decisions to invest and also to divest.

Finally, financing cash flows are the outcome of borrowing decisions, which often take the form of transactions with a bank. In Sarah's case, one of her transactions is the partial repayment of a mortgage. This is a financing cash outflow. Similarly if she were to negotiate a new mortgage, the resulting increase in her bank account would be a financing cash inflow. For a company, financing cash flows include items such as borrowing in the form of bank loans, or cash inflows from issuing new shares.

In summary, operating cash flows involve changes to wealth, while investing and financing cash flows can be viewed as wealth-neutral. For example, when Sarah receives income from her consulting work, she becomes better off. Likewise, when she consumes some of her wealth, whether at the supermarket or the cinema, she becomes worse off. On the other hand, if she buys a car, then the reduction in her bank balance is compensated by the acquisition of an asset. So long as the car is worth what she paid for it, she is neither better off nor worse off as a consequence of her investing cash outflow. Similarly, even though her bank balance would increase if she took out a new mortgage, her obligation to the bank would increase in equal measure, and so she is neither better off nor worse off even though she has more cash available to spend.

Fundamental limitations of the cash flow statement

Now let us return to the four limitations of the bank statement identified earlier. We have dealt with two of these (the presentational limitations) because, in the form of a cash flow statement, we have summarised and categorised the transactions, including separating wealth-changing transactions from wealth-neutral transactions. We will now address the two fundamental limitations.

We start by noting that the total value of Sarah's assets is greater than the amount of money she has in the bank. Alternatively stated, cash is not her only asset. In order to measure her total wealth, therefore, we need to take account of her non-cash assets, for which we need information that a cash flow statement cannot in principle provide. This is the first of the two fundamental limitations of the cash flow statement. As we shall see, the need for information concerning total wealth is met not by the cash flow statement but by the balance sheet.

Just as total wealth is not concerned with cash alone, so too a measure of the change in Sarah's total wealth must include not just the change in her bank balance but also in all of her other assets. This, then, is the second fundamental limitation of the cash flow statement, namely that cash flow is only a partial measure of changes in wealth. As we shall see, the financial statement that brings together all changes in wealth is the income statement.

We can now proceed to introduce additional information, beyond that in the bank statement in Table 2.1, concerning Sarah's financial activities. We will start with the income statement. The following is a summary of items that have changed the value of Sarah's assets and liabilities during the year, but that have not involved cash flows (i.e. they affect balance sheet items other than those in the bank account):

1. Sarah completed consulting work during the year, which remained unpaid at the year-end but which was invoiced at €2,000.
2. At the end of the year, Sarah had an outstanding council tax payment of €150.
3. The car that Sarah bought during the year had an estimated value of €6,200 at the end of the year.
4. Sarah's bike was stolen during the year. It had cost her €500.
5. Sarah estimates, based on current market values, that the market price of her house has probably increased somewhat during the year.

Before continuing to read the next paragraph, take a look at the five items above and, taking account also of the information in Sarah's cash flow statement, try to estimate how much better off Sarah has become during the course of the year. This is the same question as how much wealthier she has become, or how much her assets have increased in value, or how much profit (or surplus) she has made during the year. What you are doing, in effect, is creating an income statement.

Profit and accruals

The concept of profit is perhaps best understood as a measure of change in wealth. If an individual acquires an asset for an investment of €100, and if that asset is subsequently sold for €130, then the individual has made a profit of €30, because his or her wealth has increased from €100 to €130. In order to measure profit, therefore, we need a measure of wealth at the beginning and at the end of a period of time. If a transaction or event leads to an increase in the value of an individual's assets or, amounting to the same thing, a reduction in the value of the individual's liabilities, then he or she has made a profit. Correspondingly, a decrease in assets or an increase in liabilities results in a loss. As we will now show, this line of thinking can be applied to each of the five non-cash items listed above as, indeed, to all items that are ever reported in an income statement. We will discuss each of the five items in turn.

First, if Sarah has undertaken consulting work this year, for which she has invoiced but not yet received payment, then the question arises whether her wealth has increased this year (when the work was done) or whether instead it will increase next year (when payment will enter her bank account). In other words, does she have an asset at the end of this year as a consequence of the work she has done? The answer to this question is that we can reasonably say that she does have an asset, because her client now owes her money, which she can expect to be paid and, if necessary, for which she has the legally enforceable right to receive. In effect, she owns €2,000, and so this is the value of her asset. On the other hand, once she receives payment from her client, she will herself owe a significant part of her income, say 40 per cent, in the form of taxation. Overall, then, her unpaid work gives rise to an asset worth €2,000, an offsetting liability of €800, and overall a profit of €1,200.

In arriving at the profit of €1,200, we have applied a fundamental accounting principle known as accruals, according to which profit (or loss) is measured independently of the timing of the associated cash flow. We determined that Sarah has earned €2,000 this year, even though she will not actually receive the cash until next year. Similarly, we determined that she will have to pay tax on this income, and we have reduced her profit this year accordingly, yet this year's bank statement is unaffected.

The concept of accruals was hinted at in Chapter 1, and this chapter has also implicitly described the need for accruals accounting. In essence, if profit is a measure of change in wealth, and if cash is only one component of wealth, then profit must include changes in wealth that do not involve cash flows, and it is these changes that are termed accruals. In fact, and as we shall now see, each of the adjustments from cash flow to profit, for the five items listed above, is an example of an accrual.

Table 2.3 reports operating cash flows, accruals and profit. You can see from the first line in Table 2.3 that Sarah's total income comprises the amount received in cash (€5,700) plus her accrued income (€2,000). Similarly, her total tax expense comprises an amount paid in cash (€2,280) and an accrual (€800). The other amounts in Table 2.3 are likewise operating cash flows and accruals, which are added together to determine income and expense in the income statement.

The second of Sarah's non-cash items is, in effect, the opposite of the first. In this case, instead of earning income without having yet received payment, Sarah has incurred expenses without having yet paid for them. Instead of there being an asset, because Sarah is owed a given amount, there is instead a liability, because she owes

Table 2.3 Operating cash flow plus accruals equals profit

	Operating cash flow €	Accruals €	Income statement €
Income	5,700	2,000	7,700
Cash expenses	−1,391		−1,391
Income tax	−2,280	−800	−3,080
Council tax		−150	−150
Depreciation		−2,400	−2,400
Loss of bike		−500	−500
Profit after tax	2,029	−1,850	179

a given amount. The effect is to reduce her wealth. Even though her bank balance is unaffected, she is worse off because she now owes €150 that she previously did not owe. This amount is an accrual, or an accrued expense, and it reduces her profit.

The third item is again an accrual. When Sarah bought her car, it did not affect her wealth, as measured in the accounts, because we took the view that the amount of money that came out of her bank account was equal to the value of the car that she had purchased. By the end of the year, however, the value of her car has declined. This decline is not associated with her spending any money, and so her bank account is unaffected, but nevertheless her total wealth has fallen. Again, this decline in the asset's value, which we term depreciation, is included as an accrued expense in measuring her profit for the year.

The fourth item concerns the loss of Sarah's bike. This is very similar to the reduction in the value of the car, because in both cases the value of Sarah's assets has declined, without any corresponding cash flow, resulting in an accrued expense. This similarity holds even though the value of the bike declines to zero, while that of the car declines to a level significantly above zero. There is, however, an important difference between the two examples. In the case of the car, we are told what the asset is currently worth, while in the case of the bike, we are told only what it had cost to purchase, yet what matters to her now is the value currently attributed to the bike. If, at the time it was stolen, the bike had a value of only €100, and if this was the amount at which the bike was actually valued in Sarah's accounts, meaning that Sarah must have had accrued expenses of €400 on the bike in previous years, then the accrued expense in the current year (i.e. the value of her loss) would be only €100.

This discussion raises an important general point, namely that profit is in practice measured by reference to the asset values that are currently included in a set of accounts. If Sarah's bike had been valued at €500 in the accounts at the start of the current year, then her loss would be €500, or if €100, then €100. It follows that if, as is often the case, it is difficult to measure the value of an asset, then it is also necessarily difficult to measure profit. This is illustrated further by our final example, which is the increase in the value of the house. In this case, while we are fairly sure that the value has increased, we unfortunately do not know by how much. In a case such as this, we ignore the value change in the accounts; the accrual is zero. The effect is that while we believe Sarah to be better off, we make no allowance for this in measuring profit. We can therefore say that profit probably understates her change in wealth, and is therefore an imperfect measure, but we cannot say just how imperfect it is, because we are not actually sure of the value of her assets. This is unavoidable: the reliable measurement of profit requires the reliable measurement of assets and liabilities.

The difficulty of valuation applies in varying degrees to all items on the balance sheet, arguably with cash being the only exception. In the case of the €2,000 that Sarah is owed by her client, for example, we have implicitly assumed, in measuring her income of €2,000, that she really does have an asset that is worth that much. It might be the case, however, that the client never pays the full amount that Sarah believes she is owed, meaning that the income of €2,000 should not be regarded as an objective measure, but rather as a best case estimate of Sarah's change in wealth during the period. Similarly, Sarah's car might actually be worth €5,800 and not the estimated €6,200, in which case Sarah's assets and profit are both overstated by €400. In general, because profit is a measure of change in wealth, and because wealth can only at best be subjectively estimated, profit is necessarily to some degree a subjective measure. In this important respect, profit differs from cash flow, since there is no subjectivity concerning amounts flowing in and out of a bank account.

We can now return to calculating profit for Sarah. We have concluded that her consulting work makes her better off by €2,000, that her unpaid taxes make her worse off by €950, and that she has lost €2,400 off the value of her car. Let us also assume that she had included the value of her bike in her accounts at its original cost, in which case her loss is €500. Finally, we will not make an accrual for the change in the value of her house. If we now take all of these accruals and add them to operating cash flow (i.e. to that part of her overall cash flow that changed her wealth, as opposed to the investing and financing cash flows that were wealth-neutral), then we arrive at a measure of profit of €179, as shown in Table 2.3.

Profit is similar to cash flow in that both are measures of change during a period of time. Profit measures the change in overall wealth, while cash flow measures the change in the bank balance, which is one of the assets that comprise overall wealth. While both profit and cash flow provide useful information regarding Sarah's economic activities, they are, however, an incomplete picture because they measure only changes not levels: it is one thing to know how much the value of an asset has changed, but another to know what it was worth in the first place. This is the second fundamental limitation of the cash flow statement that was raised earlier and so, having just addressed the first limitation by means of determining an income statement, we will now address the second by means of a balance sheet.

The balance sheet

The financial statement that presents levels of wealth is the balance sheet. We have already made many direct or indirect references to the balance sheet, in this chapter and the last, not least because a proper understanding of the income statement, and indeed to some extent the cash flow statement also, requires an understanding of the balance sheet. All three financial statements are inextricably linked to one another, and a proper understanding of accounting requires an understanding not just of each individual statement but also of the linkages among them.

For any given individual or organisation (which we can term the 'reporting entity'), the balance sheet comprises two parts. On the one hand, it reports everything that is owned by the reporting entity and, on the other hand, it reports everything that is owed. Alternatively stated, it reports a list of assets and a corresponding list of the individuals or organisations to whom those assets belong. This latter group has two components: liabilities and equity. This structure is best explained with an example.

Sarah owns a house, which is an asset in her accounts. She also has a mortgage, which is a liability in her accounts. The difference between the value of her asset and the value of her mortgage is her equity, which is the share of the house that she owns herself, as opposed to that which in effect belongs to the bank. In other words,

Table 2.4 Opening balance sheet

		€
Assets	House	350,000
	Bike	500
	Bank account	8,500
	Total assets	**359,000**
Liabilities	Mortgage	220,000
	Total liabilities	**220,000**
Equity		**139,000**

the value of the asset is equal to the value of ownership claims on the asset, which are either held by third parties or by the equity holder: assets equal liabilities plus equity. The central idea is that value can be viewed simultaneously from two perspectives, namely by asking what an asset is worth or by asking what is the value of ownership claims on the asset. The balance sheet reports both perspectives, and a balance sheet must always balance because the former perspective must always be equal to the latter. If, for example, the value of Sarah's house increases while that of her mortgage stays the same, the value of her equity must have increased by exactly the same amount as the increase in the value of the house: assets are *always* equal to liabilities plus equity.

Sarah's balance sheet for the start of the financial year is shown in Table 2.4. A balance sheet reports assets, liabilities and equity at a specific point in time, and for this reason it is often referred to as a snapshot. As you saw in Chapter 1, there is one balance sheet at the start of a financial year, and another at the end. In Sarah's case, the opening balance sheet comprises only three assets, namely her house, bike and bank balance, which are in total worth €359,000. Offsetting these assets is a single liability, namely her mortgage of €220,000. Her equity (i.e. her personal net worth) is therefore €139,000, which is the value of the assets less that of the liability.

As we now have Sarah's opening balance sheet, as well as her cash flow statement and income statement, we are in a position to determine her closing balance sheet, which will give us a complete set of her financial statements. Before reading the next section, have a go at trying to produce the closing balance sheet. This will require starting with the opening balance sheet, and going through each of the items in the cash flow statement and the income statement, working out in each case what impact they have on the amounts in the balance sheet. A centrally important guide for completing this exercise is to note that each transaction or event affects two items on the balance sheet, simultaneously and by an equal amount. For example, the purchase of a car affects two assets, the car and the bank balance. Equally, the capital repayment on the mortgage causes a reduction in an asset (bank balance) that is equal to a reduction in a liability (mortgage). As a final example, expenses incurred by visiting the coffee shop reduce an asset (bank balance) and also equity. The reason why, in this case, it is equity that is affected, rather than an asset or a liability, is as follows. Only one of Sarah's assets is affected by the coffee purchase, namely her bank balance, and so the overall value of her assets has declined. This being the case, the corresponding value of the claims on those assets must also have declined. Given that, in this case, the value of claims represented by liabilities has not changed, it must be the value of the equity claim that has declined. Intuitively, Sarah had a sum of money that has now been spent on a consumable item, as a result of which her net worth is reduced.

You should note that, in each of three examples just described – the purchase of a car, the repayment of a mortgage, or the consumption of coffee – the method of accounting starts by asking what the impact is on the balance sheet, and in particular which two balance sheet items are affected. You should therefore follow this approach in determining Sarah's closing balance sheet.

As a further guide in completing this exercise, it will be helpful to summarise the nature of the relationships between, on the one hand, the income statement and the cash flow statement (i.e. the two statements concerned with changes in asset values over time) and, on the other hand, the balance sheet (i.e. the statement concerned with asset values themselves at a point in time). Specifically, profit measures the change in equity between the opening and closing balance sheets, while cash flow measures the change in the bank balance. Corresponding to the opening and closing balance sheets, there is a single income statement and a single cash flow statement, each of which reports changes between the two balance sheet dates. It is in the balance sheet that everything comes together: the income statement and the cash flow statement both report changes in specific items on the balance sheet, while differences between the income statement and the cash flow statement can be explained by differences in other items on the balance sheet. For example, when Sarah purchased a car, there was a cash flow that reduced her bank

Table 2.5 Piecing together all of Sarah's financial activities

		Opening €	Cash €	Accrual €	Closing €
Assets	House	350,000			350,000
	Car	0	8 600	−2,400	6,200
	Bike	500		−500	0
	Accounts receivable	0		2,000	2,000
	Bank account	8,500	−7,571		929
		359,000	1,029	−900	359,129
Liabilities	Mortgage	220,000	−1,000		219,000
	Tax payable	0		950	950
		220,000	−1,000	950	219,950
Equity		139,000	2,029	−1,850	139,179

balance, but there was no profit or loss because the account for her car was increased, and there was no overall effect on the value of assets. Once the car starts to depreciate, there will be a reduction in the value of assets and a corresponding expense, but no effect on cash flow. In short, if the workings of the balance sheet are properly understood, then it follows that the income statement and the cash flow statement are understood also, because in accounting all transactions and events impact the balance sheet. This is all best understood by means of a worked example, so you should now try to complete Sarah's closing balance sheet before reading the next section.

Linkages among the financial statements

In order to help explain how Sarah's closing balance sheet is derived, Table 2.5 sets out all of the linkages among Sarah's financial statements. This looks complicated at first sight, because in effect it pulls together all the content of the chapter into a single place. The first and final columns of numbers report her opening and closing balance sheets, respectively, while the second column shows the impact on the balance sheet of all items in her cash flow statement, and the third column shows the impact of accruals.

It will be helpful, in order to reinforce your understanding of the structure of the financial statements, to go carefully through each of the rows in Table 2.5. As we do this, you will see that the same underlying logic and structure is in effect being repeated over and over, albeit in a somewhat different form in each case. You should see the following as a consolidation of Chapters 1 and 2.

1. Sarah's house was valued at €350,000 in the opening balance sheet. There were no cash transactions regarding the house during the year (i.e. no investing cash flows) and neither was the value of the house revised in the accounts (i.e. no accruals), meaning that the house remains valued at £350,000 in the closing balance sheet.

2. Sarah had no car at the start of the year, but she then acquired a car for €8,600 in cash, and she subsequently revised this value to account for €2,400 of depreciation, making the closing balance sheet value €6,200. This €2,400 is an accrual because it changes the value of her net assets (i.e. it affects profit) but it does not involve a cash flow.

3. Sarah had a bike at the start of the year, which was valued in her accounts at €500. During the year, it was stolen, and so the value of her net assets reduced by €500. As with depreciation, this €500 is an accrual because it changes the value of her net assets (i.e. it affects profit) but it does not involve a cash flow.

4. The asset 'accounts receivable' (otherwise known as 'debtors') refers to amounts invoiced where the cash has not yet been received. In Sarah's case, there were no accounts receivable in the opening balance sheet, but during the year she invoiced €2,000 to her client, which remained unpaid at the year end. She therefore has an accrual of €2,000 and a closing balance of €2,000.

5. The bank account line in Table 2.5 is, in effect, the cash flow statement. It shows the opening bank balance, the total cash flow during the year and the closing bank balance. If we examine the cash column in Table 2.5, we can see the distinction between, on the one hand, operating cash flow and, on the other hand, investing and financing cash flow. The total change in cash (−€7,571) is the sum of all three types of cash flow. The investing cash flow (−€8,600) appears in Table 2.5 as an increase in one asset (car) and a decrease in another (bank balance). The financing cash flow (−€1,000) appears as a decrease in a liability (mortgage) and a decrease in an asset (bank balance). Neither the investing cash flow nor the financing cash flow affects equity, because in both cases the overall value of assets less liabilities remains the same: Sarah's wealth neither increases nor decreases. In contrast, the operating cash flow (€2,029) appears in Table 2.5 as an increase in an asset (bank balance) and a corresponding increase

Table 2.6 Sarah's summary financial statements

			€
Cash flow statement	Operating		2,029
	Investing		−8,600
	Financing		−1,000
	Change in cash		**−7,571**
	Opening balance		8,500
	Closing balance		929
Income statement	Income		7,700
	Expense		−7,521
	Profit		**179**
Balance sheet	**Assets**	House	350,000
		Car	6,200
		Accounts receivable	2,000
		Bank account	929
	Total assets		**359,129**
	Liabilities	Mortgage	219,000
		Tax payable	950
			219,950
	Equity		**139,179**

in equity. This is because the net inflow of cash from operating activity simply makes Sarah better off.

6. Sarah started the year with a mortgage of €220,000, against which she has made a capital repayment in cash of €1,000, leaving her with an outstanding liability of €219,000 at the end of the year.

7. At the start of the year, Sarah did not owe any tax, but during the course of the year she has incurred a liability for income tax of €800 and for council tax of €150. She therefore has a total accrual of €950, which reduces both her personal net worth and her profit.

8. The change to the equity line in Table 2.5 is, in effect, the income statement. Sarah's personal net worth at the start of the year was €139,000. She generated €2,029 operating cash flow during the year and incurred €1,850 in accrued expenses, giving her a profit of €179 and so a closing equity balance of €139,179. If we examine the accruals column in Table 2.5, we can see that, taken together, the four accruals affecting the car, bike, accounts receivable and tax payable reduce Sarah's wealth by €1,850, which is equal to

the change in equity resulting from accruals (as also shown in Table 2.3). This is because, for each of these four items, the method of accounting was to change, on the one hand, the value of the asset or liability and, on the other hand, the value of equity. So, for example, the reduction in the value of the bike of €500 corresponded to a reduction in equity of €500.

In summary

We have seen, based upon exploring the simple example of Sarah's economic activity, that we have a need for three primary financial statements – the cash flow statement, income statement and balance sheet – and that these provide a useful summary of economic activity for Sarah, as, indeed, they would also provide for a commercial organisation or other entity. Each of these statements is provided in summary form in Table 2.6.

We can now answer the four questions that we posed at the start.

• How wealthy is Sarah?

At the end of the financial year, our estimate of Sarah's personal net worth is €139,179. We regard this as an estimate because we cannot be entirely sure that we have a reliable valuation for her house, car and accounts receivable.

• Does Sarah have debts and is she able to pay them?

Sarah's total debts (or liabilities) amount to €219,950, made up of a large mortgage and a relatively small amount of tax payable. Sarah appears to have no problem at the present time in being able to pay her debts. Most of her tax (€800) is only payable after she has received €2,000 from her client, and the remaining €150 is comfortably covered by her bank balance of €929. Meanwhile, the value of her house greatly exceeds that of her mortgage, implying that she has not borrowed too heavily.

• Was Sarah's income greater than her expenditure over the course of the past year?

Sarah's income last year was marginally higher than her expenditure, giving her a profit of €179 over the course of the year.

• Can Sarah afford to maintain her current level of spending?

Sarah's profit is small in relation to her income, meaning that over the past year she has only just been able to live within her means. Whether or not she will be able to continue to live within her means will depend upon the sustainability of her income and of her expenditure. If we assume that she will continue to earn her consulting income at the same level, then it is the sustainability of her expenditure that we need to focus on. Here, the news is encouraging. Her profit this year has been reduced by €500 because of the loss of her bike. As this is likely to be a one-off loss, we can expect (other things being equal) that her profit next year would be €679 rather than €179. Moreover, it is likely that the depreciation on her car in its second year will be lower than that experienced in the first year, making her overall expenses lower still and her profit higher. If Sarah's income can be sustained, then it seems safe to conclude that she can comfortably afford to maintain her current level of spending.

3 | Keeping track of economic activity

Keeping track of economic activity

Chapter 1 presented an overview of the financial statements, which was extended in Chapter 2 with an intuitive exploration of why we have a cash flow statement, income statement and balance sheet and of how each of these statements is related to one another. In this chapter, the aim is to consolidate your understanding, which we will do by examining the underlying mechanisms of accounting, the so-called 'double-entry' system by which economic activity is captured and portrayed in a set of financial statements.

The notion that we are consolidating, rather than extending, understanding is actually very important. Financial accounting can be described as comprising a single model for measuring financial position and financial performance. This model, which is based on the double-entry method and which includes, as we have seen, the balance sheet, income statement and cash flow statement, is effectively all that there is to financial accounting. Financial position is measured in terms of assets, liabilities and equity, and financial performance is measured in terms of changes in these items. There is nothing else to it. Every single transaction or event that is captured in a set of financial statements can be described in terms of its impact on financial position and, so, on financial performance. It does not matter whether we are dealing with revenue, operating expenses, taxation, fixed assets, accounts receivable, dividends, bank loans or the acquisition of one business by another: all of these things are captured in terms of their impact on the balance sheet, the income statement and the cash flow statement.

Understanding financial accounting is therefore all about getting your mind around a single model. This is good news. Moreover, the accounting model is truly universal. It is used across all sectors of the economy and in all parts of the world. If you grasp the essentials of the model, then you are in a position to understand the accounting treatment of any item whatsoever in the financial statements of any organisation.

The challenge is that the accounting model is unlike anything else and requires a method of thinking that is typically not intuitive. At first sight, the model is confusing to most people. Moreover, because all elements of the model are interconnected, it is not possible to really understand what is going on without being able to fit all of the pieces together. A common experience in learning accounting is to find that while some elements of the model seem to make sense, others do not, and an understanding of the whole feels elusive. Going through this experience is a natural part of learning. The good news is that once all of the fundamentals of the model are in place, and it no longer feels counter-intuitive but instead makes sense, then everything becomes much easier. Accounting is not a subject that starts easy and gradually becomes more difficult as you learn more; it is the opposite. It is a challenge to get your mind around the meaning of the financial statements and the relationships that each has to one another, but having got over this initial hurdle, you are entitled to feel that you have arrived. Hence, while the material here is only introductory, it is really much more fundamental: if you can become really fluent with the concepts presented here, then you will understand the essence of any advanced textbook or complex set of financial statements.

You may recall from the worked example of Sarah's accounts in Chapter 2 that, for each transaction and event, you were asked to consider the impact on the balance sheet, and in particular which two balance sheet items were affected. In general, and as the following discussion of double entry will show, it is the balance sheet that is at the heart of a fluent understanding of accounting. This is because all transactions and events recorded in the financial statements are best described first and foremost in terms of their impact on the balance sheet. Even the income statement and the cash flow statement are best described in terms of changes between one balance sheet and another. This point will become clearer as you read on in this chapter.

In summary, therefore, we will start the chapter with the balance sheet and aim to consolidate your understanding of the structure of the financial statements. We will discuss what causes balance sheet values to change, and what the implications of these changes are for the income statement and the cash flow statement. We will then progress from concept to practice, by exploring the mechanics of double-entry accounting. By the end of the chapter, you should be able to create a set of financial statements from any basic set of transactions and events, and you should be able to describe how the amounts in each of the financial statements are related to one another.

Table 3.1 Impact of Sarah's transactions and events on the balance sheet

Salary (cash)	Cash↑	Equity↑
Expenses (cash)	Equity↓	Cash↓
Acquisition of car	PPE↑	Cash↓
Mortgage repayment	Mortgage↓	Cash↓
Salary (accrued)	Accounts receivable↑	Equity↑
Depreciation	Equity↓	PPE↓
Loss of bike	Equity↓	PPE↓
Accrued tax	Equity↓	Tax payable↑

Balance sheet

As we have seen, there are three components to the balance sheet: assets, liabilities and equity. Assets are items of value that belong to the entity. Liabilities and equity are both ownership claims on these items of value. A balance sheet must always balance, in the sense that assets must be equal to liabilities plus equity, because the total value of an entity's assets must be equal to the total value of the ownership claim on those assets.

The balance sheet measures financial position at a point in time, and there is one balance sheet at the beginning of a reporting period and another at the end. Fundamental to an understanding of accounting is knowing what causes the balance sheet to change between two periods of time, and in particular understanding how and why different types of change to the balance sheet differ from one another.

As a simple illustration, Table 3.1 summarises the changes to the balance sheet that arose in the earlier example of Sarah's financial statements.

Several important observations can be made from Table 3.1.

- Every transaction or event impacts the balance sheet in two places, which is the reason for the term 'double entry'. For example, the purchase of the car impacts two assets (car and cash), the mortgage repayment impacts an asset and a liability (cash and mortgage), and depreciation impacts an asset (property, plant and equipment (PPE)) and equity. By ensuring that each change to one part of the balance sheet is matched by another change of equal amount to another part, double entry is the mechanism by which a balance sheet always balances, meaning that the value of assets must be equal to that of liabilities plus equity.

- If either of the two balance items impacted is equity, then this affects profit. For example, Sarah's consulting activities provides her with income, which increases profit, while depreciation of her car results in an expense, which reduces profit.
- If either of the two balance sheet items impacted is cash, then there is a cash flow. If the corresponding entry is to an asset (or a liability) other than cash, with no overall effect on net assets and so no change in equity, then the cash flow is either investing or financing. For example, Sarah's acquisition of a car is an investing cash flow, because the two accounts affected are PPE and cash, while the mortgage repayment is a financing cash flow, because the two accounts affected are mortgage and cash. In contrast, if the corresponding entry is to equity, for example when Sarah receives her consulting income in cash, then the change in cash is an operating cash flow.
- Although each item in Table 3.1 affects either cash, or equity, or both, Sarah could in principle have a transaction that affects neither equity nor cash. For example, if she had bought furniture on credit, then she would have a new asset (furniture) and a corresponding new liability (accounts payable), with no effect on either profit (because net assets are unchanged and so she is neither better nor worse off) or on cash (because she has not yet paid for the furniture).

In summary, when a transaction or event is recognised in the financial statements, there are always two changes to the balance sheet. We can categorise these changes in terms of three distinct components of the balance sheet: equity, net assets excluding cash, and cash. The reason for this categorisation is that it corresponds to the primary financial statements. The cash flow statement reports changes in cash, and so it is necessary to separate cash as a distinct component of the balance sheet. Similarly, the income statement reports changes in equity, and so equity is also a distinct component. The remainder of the balance sheet, having separated out equity and cash, is net assets excluding cash (i.e. total assets excluding cash less total liabilities).

Take a look at Table 3.2, which in effect repeats Table 3.1 but does so by describing each double entry in terms of its impact on each

Table 3.2 Summary of changes to Sarah's balance sheet

Salary (cash)	Cash↑	Equity↑
Expenses (cash)	Equity↓	Cash↓
Acquisition of car	Net assets (excluding cash)↑	Cash↓
Mortgage repayment	Net assets (excluding cash)↑	Cash↓
Salary (accrued)	Net assets (excluding cash)↑	Equity↑
Depreciation	Equity↓	Net assets (excluding cash)↓
Loss of bike	Equity↓	Net assets (excluding cash)↓
Accrued tax	Equity↓	Net assets (excluding cash) ↓

of the three categories summarised above. As you go through each line, you will see that what is being described is which of the financial statements is being affected by each double entry. This is a helpful exercise in framing your understanding of the balance sheet and the double-entry system.

Table 3.3 captures all of this in a systematic way, by summarising the different possibilities that exist under double-entry accounting. Each of the four boxes in Table 3.3 represents different ways in which any given double-entry affects the financial statements. Reading clockwise, double entries in the first box impact equity and cash, while those in the second box impact equity but not cash, those in the third box impact neither equity nor cash and, finally, those in the fourth box affect cash but not equity. This is all there is. Apart from certain changes within equity, which need not concern us here, everything in accounting is captured by the four categories in Table 3.3.

Within two of the categories, there are two possibilities, and so, in total, Table 3.3 captures six different ways in which any given double entry affects the financial statements. Each of these will now be discussed in turn. You can use the following as a checklist. If you are required to complete a double entry, or if you simply want to understand why any given double entry has been made or, more generally, if you want to understand what goes on behind the scenes in creating a set of financial statements, then the following provides a

Table 3.3 Changes to the balance sheet

	Cash	Net assets excluding cash
Equity	1. Operating cash flow 2. Financing cash flow (transactions with shareholders)	3. Accruals
Net assets excluding cash	5. Financing cash flow (excluding transactions with shareholders) 6. Investing cash flow	4. Offsetting changes within net assets

concise yet exhaustive list of possibilities. As you go through this list, keep a mental picture of the basic structure of a balance sheet, and in each case work through in your mind the effect of the double entry.

1. *Operating cash flow (change to equity and cash)*

Examples: sales for which payment is in cash; payment of expenses in cash.

If there is an increase or depletion of the asset of cash, but the values of other assets and liabilities remain unchanged, then there is an overall change in net assets and, therefore a change in equity (i.e. either a profit or a loss). This is an operating cash flow.

2. *Shareholder financing cash flow (change to equity and cash)*

Examples: issue of new shares for cash; cash payment of dividends; cash buy-back of shares.

If there is a cash transaction between the company and its shareholders, for example when a dividend is paid, then this will change both equity and cash. In the case of a dividend, the effect of the payment is to reduce cash and, because no other asset or liability is affected, to reduce net assets also. In the same way as an operating cash flow, the result of there being fewer net assets is that the value of the shareholders' stake in the business has reduced. In sharp contrast with operating cash flow, however, shareholders are not worse off as a consequence of this reduction in net assets, because they have received a cash payment exactly equal to the reduction in net assets. Similarly, shareholders are not better off if an increase in net assets results from a cash payment from the shareholders to the company whenever new shares are issued. The value of equity therefore changes for two reasons: first, whenever there is a profit or a loss and, second, whenever there are transactions between the company and its shareholders. Therefore, profit can be defined as the change in equity excluding transactions with shareholders. You should note that this refines somewhat our earlier definition of profit (which was simply that profit is equal to a change in equity). So, for example, if a company makes a profit of €300 but also pays a dividend of €50, then equity increases by €250. Hence profit is not the change in equity, but instead the change in equity excluding the dividend payment, which is a transaction with shareholders.

3. Accruals (change to equity but not to cash)

Examples: credit sales; depreciation; write-down of assets, for example if plant and equipment becomes obsolete, if inventory is damaged or if accounts receivable are deemed to be uncollectible; expenses incurred before being paid for in cash.

As we have already seen, operating cash flow alone does not measure financial performance. This is because cash is only one part of net assets. Financial performance concerns changes in the value of all assets and liabilities, not just cash. These non-cash changes in net assets are called accruals. In some cases, accruals arise because the value on the balance sheet of an existing asset or a liability is revised. This revision is downwards if, for example, an asset has depreciated, causing a reduction in equity. Similarly, if the liability of tax payable is initially under-estimated, and if a revision is made to increase the liability, then the effect of the revision is to reduce net assets and, so, equity. In contrast, an accrual will lead to an increase in equity if, for example, there is a recognised increase in the market value of a portfolio of financial investments. Accruals can also arise when a new asset or liability is created. In such cases, income or expense is recognised in advance of the cash flow taking place. The most obvious example is sales made on credit, where the effect is to increase accounts receivable and equity. Similarly, if expenses are incurred and cash settlement has not yet taken place, then the accounting treatment is to create a liability and reduce equity.

4. Offsetting changes within net assets (change to neither equity nor cash)

Examples: purchase of inventory on credit; leasing, whereby the acquisition of PPE is financed by a loan from the leasing company, with no cash changing hands.

In some cases, a transaction or event has no effect on either profit or cash. For example, if a supplier provides inventory, this will typically increase the asset of inventory and the liability of accounts payable. In this case, the increase in the asset is offset by the increase in the liability, and there is no change in net assets and therefore no effect on profit.

5. *Non-shareholder financing cash flow (changes to cash but not to equity)*

Examples: cash received when a new bank loan is raised; cash paid in full or partial settlement of an existing bank loan.
If an inflow of cash corresponds to an equal and simultaneous depletion of assets or increase in liabilities, shareholders' wealth does not change, and vice versa. In other words, if there is no overall change in net assets, then neither is there a change in equity. Financing cash flows fall into this category. For example, if a new bank loan is raised, or if an existing loan is settled, then the change in the value of liabilities is equal to the simultaneous change in cash.

6. *Investing cash flow (changes to cash but not to equity)*

Examples: cash purchase of PPE; cash received from the disposal of PPE.
Investing cash flows are similar to financing cash flows in that they are changes in cash that are not associated with changes in equity. The difference is that investing cash flows involve the acquisition and disposal of assets, while financing cash flows concern raising and repaying debt. If a change in an asset, such as a building, occurs simultaneously with a change in cash, then there is an investing cash flow. Specifically, an increase in assets such as buildings corresponds to negative investing cash flow, and vice versa.

Table 3.4 provides an illustration of all six of these types of double entry. The illustration starts with an opening balance sheet, progresses through each of the six types of change to the balance sheet, and then concludes with a closing balance sheet.

You should test your understanding by examining each column in Table 3.4. To help in this process, the following is a summary of each of the double entries.

1. Cash of €10 is spent on operating expenses. There is no impact on any component of net assets other than cash. Equity/profit decline by €10.
2. A dividend of €2 is paid. Cash reduces by €2. There is no impact on any component of net assets other than cash. Equity declines by €2

Table 3.4 Different types of change to the balance sheet

| | Opening balance sheet € | Changes to the balance sheet | | | | | | Closing Balance Sheet € |
		1 Operating cash flow €	2 Shareholder financing cash flow €	3 Accrual €	4 Offsetting changes within net assets €	5 Non-shareholder financing cash flow €	6 Investing cash flow €	
PPE	150			−5			5	150
Inventory	0				15			15
Accounts receivable	40			25				65
Cash	20	−10	−2			35	−5	38
Assets	**210**	**−10**	**−2**	**20**	**15**	**35**	**0**	**268**
Bank loan	70					35		105
Accounts payable	30				15			45
Liabilities	**100**	**0**	**0**	**0**	**15**	**35**	**0**	**150**
Net assets	**110**	**−10**	**−2**	**20**	**0**	**35**	**0**	**118**
Share capital	100							100
Retained profit	10	−10	−2	20				18
Equity	**110**	**−10**	**−2**	**20**	**0**	**0**	**0**	**118**

but there is no effect on profit earned during the year, because this is a transaction with shareholders; it is retained profit that declines.

3. There are two double entries made here. The first is depreciation, which reduces the book value of PPE by €5. The second is revenue, which increases accounts receivable by €25. In both cases, shareholders have become better off but there has been no transaction in cash. Both cases are therefore examples of accruals. Together, they increase the value of net assets by €20, so increasing equity by €20.

4. Inventory is provided by a supplier, which increases the value of assets by €15. The inventory is supplied on credit, so instead of a reduction in cash to pay for the inventory, there is a new liability of €15. The increase in assets is offset by an increase in liabilities, and so there is no change in net assets. Overall, therefore, there is no change in either cash or equity.

5. A new bank loan of €35 is raised, creating a new liability. As the asset of cash increases by the same amount as the liability, there is no change in net assets and so no change in equity. As the source of the change in cash is a bank loan, this is a financing cash flow.

6. A new item of PPE is purchased in cash, creating a new asset with a book value of €5. As the asset of cash reduces by the same amount, there is no change in net assets and so no change in equity. As the source of the change in cash is the purchase of an asset, this is an investing cash flow.

Overall, retained profit increases by €8, which is a profit of €10 less a dividend of €2. The profit was comprised of operating cash flow of –€10 plus accruals of €20. The change in cash was €18, made up of operating cash flow of –€10, investing cash flow of –€5 to acquire PPE, and financing cash flow of €33 (a bank loan of €35, less a dividend payment of €2).

Debits, credits, journal entries and the general ledger

We have seen that the process of accounting always progresses by means of double entry. Given that double entries are therefore the fundamental building blocks in accounting, it will deepen our understanding to explore briefly how these entries are recorded and aggregated in practice to create a full set of accounts.

There are in essence two elements to the accountant's system. The first is to express each double entry in the form of what is termed a journal entry comprising a debit and a credit. The second is to construct individual accounts in such a way that all of the debit and credit amounts are aggregated into a balance sheet, income statement and cash flow statement. To explain the system further, we therefore need to define the terms debit and credit, explain how a journal entry is made, and describe how the structure of individual accounts aggregates into the financial statements.

All of this sounds more complicated than it really is. Actually, we have already in effect defined debits and credits, and so the good news is that the difficult part is already done. If you look back at Table 3.1, you will see two columns describing changes to Sarah's balance sheet. All of the items in the first of these columns are conventionally described as debit entries, and all of those in the second column as credit entries. All double entries comprise a debit entry and a credit entry of equal amounts.

The terms debit and credit are in fact just a shorthand way of summarising each of the columns in Table 3.1: a debit is an increase in assets, a decrease in liabilities or a decrease in equity; a credit is a decrease in assets, an increase in liabilities or an increase in equity. The terms DR and CR are in turn shorthand for debit and credit. This is nothing new. It is simply a different, more concise way than we have used so far to describe items in the accounts.

There is in practice a common source of confusion with the terms debit and credit. A bank balance that is positive is often described as being 'in credit'. But if your bank tells you that your account is in credit, then it is describing its side of the story, not yours. You have an asset, in the form of cash held at the bank, but the bank has a liability, because the cash that it holds belongs to you. Your asset is a debit balance, and the bank's obligation to repay you is a credit balance.

A journal entry is a simultaneous debit and credit entry made in the accounts. In the days when all accounting records were physically held in books, or journals, it made sense to describe the act of recording a double entry as a journal entry, and the name has stuck. The same is true, by the way, for other items of accounting terminology, such as book value, general ledger, writing-off an asset or booking an invoice. So, for example, Sarah would have made the following journal entry when she purchased her car (in words, she 'debited car' and 'credited cash').

	DR	CR
Car	8,000	
Cash		8,000

For each individual asset and liability, and for each separate type of income, expense or cash flow, an entity will keep a separate account. Any given journal entry will therefore affect two of these accounts. So, for example, an entity may have five different suppliers of inventories, and eight different product types that it holds in inventory. It will therefore have 13 individual accounts relating to suppliers and inventory. The debit component of a journal entry might therefore increase the book value for a specific product type, while the credit component increases the liability for accounts payable to a specific supplier, as follows.

	DR	CR
Inventory (Product X)	1,300	
Accounts Payable (Supplier Y)		1,300

The individual account for any given product maintains a record of the level of inventory at the beginning of the accounting period (a debit balance), additions to the inventory during the period (debit entries), reductions during the period (credit entries) and, so, the closing debit balance at the end of the period. Similarly, all supplier accounts will start with a credit balance, and they will increase as credit entries are made, and decrease with debit entries. These relationships are all illustrated in the example in Table 3.5, which shows one account for inventory and another for accounts payable. These accounts are commonly termed 'T-accounts' because this describes their layout, as indicated in Table 3.5. By convention, debit entries are reported on the left-hand side of a T-account, and credit entries on the right.

You should notice the following about Table 3.5:

- The opening balance, which is a debit for an asset (inventory) and a credit for a liability (accounts payable), is the amount that would appear on the opening balance sheet. If, for example, an entity has several individual accounts for different items of inventory, then the amount on the balance sheet would simply be the sum of each of these accounts. Hence, the financial statements – the balance sheet, income statement and cash flow statement – report aggregate amounts based upon a large number of underlying individual accounts.
- The first entries in the reporting period for the two accounts are each part of the same journal entry: the debit entry of €1,300 is an increase in inventory, and the credit entry of €1,300 is an increase in accounts payable.

Table 3.5 'T' accounts

	Inventory (Product X)	
	DR	CR
Opening balance	1,200	
Delivery from supplier	1,300	
Transfer to income statement		1,800
Closing balance	700	
	Accounts payable (Supplier Y)	
	DR	CR
Opening balance		500
Delivery of inventory		1,300
Cash payment	800	
Closing balance	1,000	

- The second entries for the two accounts are unrelated. In the case of inventory, there is a credit entry of €1,800, because this is the amount of inventory that was sold during the period. The debit entry in this case is a reduction in equity. In the case of accounts payable, there is a debit entry of 800, because this is the amount that was paid to the supplier during the period. The credit entry in this case is a reduction in cash.
- The closing balance for each account, which will appear on the closing balance sheet, is simply the opening balance plus the entries for the year. For an asset, debit entries increase the closing balance, and credit entries reduce it, and vice versa for a liability.

'General ledger' is the term used for the entirety of the individual accounts of an entity. This is illustrated in Table 3.6, which develops the analysis from Chapter 2 of Sarah's accounts, by setting out all of her double-entries in the form of her general ledger. You can see in Table 3.6 a lot of information coming together in a single place. In particular, you should notice the following.

- The opening balance for assets is a debit, and for equity and all liabilities it is a credit.
- The first line in Table 3.6 is simply Sarah's opening balance sheet, and the final line is her closing balance sheet.
- Each line in Table 3.6 is a journal entry. The effect of depreciation, for example, is a debit of €2,400 to equity and a credit of €2,400 to

Table 3.6 Sarah's general ledger

€	Equity		Mortgage		Tax payable		House		Bike		Car		Accounts receivable		Cash	
	DR	CR	DR	CR	DR	CR	DR	CR	DR	CR	DR	CR	DR	CR	DR	CR
Opening balance		139,000		220,000		0	350,000		500		0				8,500	
Operating cash inflow		5,700													5,700	
Operating cash: consumables	415															415
Operating cash: travel	336															336
Operating cash: leisure	138															138
Operating cash: interest	503															503
Operating cash: tax	2,280															2,280
Investing cash flow											8,600					8,600
Financing cash flow			1,000													1,000

Table 3.6 (cont.)

€	Equity		Mortgage		Tax payable		House		Bike		Car		Accounts receivable		Cash	
	DR	CR	DR	CR	DR	CR	DR	CR	DR	CR	DR	CR	DR	CR	DR	CR
Accrual: consulting income		2,000											2,000			
Accrual: depreciation	2,400											2,400				
Accrual: loss of bike	500									500						
Accrual: income tax	800					800										
Accrual: council tax	150					150										
Closing balance		139,179		219,000		950	350,000		0		6,200		2,000		929	

the car. (The operating cash flows are actually the aggregate of the individual transactions that were reported on the bank statement.)

• Each account captures changes during the year in a specific component of assets, liabilities or equity. For example, Sarah did not owe any tax at the start of the year, but a credit entry of €950 during the year leaves her with a liability of €950 at the end of the year.

• The difference between Sarah's opening cash balance of €8,500 and her closing cash balance of €929 is –€7,571. This is her cash flow for the year: it is the bottom line of her cash flow statement. It is the opening balance in her cash account, plus the sum of all debit entries, less all of the credit entries.

• The difference between the opening balance of Sarah's equity, €139,000, and the closing balance, €139,179, is her profit during the year. It is the sum of all credit entries in equity, less all of the debit entries.

There is quite a lot to Table 3.6. It is worth spending some time making sure that you understand everything that is going on.

Worked example: consulting firm general ledger

You were earlier promised that you would be able to create a set of financial statements from any basic set of transactions and events. Now here is a test of that promise!

You are asked to prepare the accounts for a consulting firm. You should first create a general ledger, in the same form as Table 3.6. You should then make each journal entry for the firm directly into the general ledger, following which you should generate a balance sheet, income statement and a cash flow statement.

The information that you need is as follows.

• At the beginning of the year (1 Jan), the firm has share capital of €100 and cash of €100.

• The firm completes two projects during the year. The first, worth €90, is invoiced to the client and then subsequently paid during the year. The second, worth €60, is invoiced during the year but remains unpaid at the end of the year.

• The firm's consultants are paid €130 during the year.

• The firm's profits are taxable at 40 per cent. No tax is paid during the year.

The answer is provided in Tables 3.7 and 3.8 but you should avoid looking at these before attempting your own answer!

Table 3.7 Consulting firm's general ledger

€	Capital		Profit		Tax due		Accounts receivable		Cash	
	DR	CR	DR	CR	DR	CR	DR	CR	DR	CR
Opening balance		100							100	
Revenue from Contract 1				90			90			
Revenue from Contract 2				60			60			
Cash from Contract 1								90	90	
Salary payments			130							130
Tax payable			8			8				
Closing balance		100		12		8	60		60	

Table 3.8 Consulting firm's financial statements

			€	€
Cash flow statement	Operating			−40
	Investing			0
	Financing			0
	Change in cash			**−40**
Income statement	Income			150
	Expense			130
	Profit before Tax			20
	Tax			8
	Profit			**12**
			1 Jan	31 Dec
Balance sheets	Assets	Accounts receivable	0	60
		Cash	100	60
			100	120
	Liabilities	Tax payable	0	8
	Net assets		**100**	**112**
	Equity	Share capital	100	100
		Retained profit	0	12
			100	**112**

In summary

While the focus of Chapter 2 was on understanding the nature of financial statement information, this chapter has reviewed how the financial statements are put together. In particular, we have explored the double-entry system, which is at the very heart of an understanding of accounting. Every set of accounts that you are likely to come across will have double entry as its foundation.

You should keep in mind that, without exception, all of the economic activity represented in the financial statements is captured via a journal entry, and each journal entry is described by one of the six options in Table 3.3. In other words, the basic building blocks in accounting are few in number and actually fairly simple. An implication for you in learning accounting is that you should always try to keep things simple. There is nothing in accounting that cannot be traced back to a journal entry, with a debit affecting one part of the balance sheet and a credit affecting another. Whenever any aspect of accounting feels complicated or confusing, going back to the underlying logic behind the double entry, and describing it as simply as possible, will be very helpful in making sense of what is going on.

4 Summary of the foundations of accounting

Summary of the foundations of accounting

In the first three chapters of this book, we have covered the foundations of accounting. Chapter 1 provided a high-level overview of the financial statements. Chapter 2 added depth by explaining the need for a balance sheet, income statement (profit and loss account) and cash flow statement, and by exploring how each of these statements is related to one another and what information each of them provides. Finally, Chapter 3 explained the nuts and bolts of accounting, providing insight into where the numbers come from and how they are fitted together.

The aim of this final chapter of Part I of the book is to consolidate your understanding. The approach will be for you to have a go at preparing a set of accounts. There is no new material in this chapter. Rather, the aim is to help you to make sure that everything in Part I has come together, and that you have built a solid foundation in accounting.

Before starting the worked example, it will first be helpful to summarise briefly the essential features of the accounting model, and to recall the limited number of ways in which *all* transactions and events are recorded in accounting.

- Every transaction or event affects the balance sheet in two places. This is double-entry accounting. Your first task will be to identify, in every case, the two individual accounts on the balance sheet that are affected. These accounts might relate, for example, to land, buildings, equipment, inventory, cash, accounts payable, bank loans, retained profits or share capital. Each one of the accounts records either assets, liabilities or equity.
- The effect of the double-entry on the total value of assets must always be the same as its effect on the total value of liabilities plus equity, and you should always ensure that this is the case. So, for example, if the asset of cash is reduced in order to purchase another asset, such as some equipment, there is no change in the overall value of assets, and neither is there a change in the overall value of liabilities plus equity. If, however, cash was spent on a

consumable item, such as travel, then there would be an expense (which reduces equity) and so the total reduction in assets would be equal to the total reduction in liabilities plus equity.

- Two of the individual accounts on the balance sheet are given a special treatment in accounting. These accounts are cash (which is an asset) and retained profit (which is a component of equity). The special treatment is that these two individual accounts are given their own financial statement. The cash flow statement is a complete record of all amounts of cash flowing in and out of the organisation during the reporting period. The income statement is a complete record of income earned and expenses incurred by the organisation during the reporting period.
- The cash flow statement is classified into three categories: operating, investing and financing.
- The income statement comprises income less expenses, which equals profit or loss and is the change in shareholders' wealth resulting from changes in net assets.

Worked example: Production Company

Production Company was founded with a €100,000 (€100k) cash investment by shareholders. Its opening balance sheet therefore comprises cash of €100k and equity of €100k.

During its first year of business, the transactions and events for Production Company were as follows.

1. Purchased van for €20k.
2. Purchased inventory for €50k.
3. Borrowed €50k from the bank.
4. Spent €15k on advertising.
5. Paid employees €25k.
6. Sold all inventory for €125k in cash.
7. Received €80k of inventory from suppliers, without having paid for it yet.
8. Sold €40k of inventory on credit for €105k.
9. Paid suppliers €20k.
10. Received €65k cash from customers.
11. Van depreciates to €16k.
12. Paid €90k in rent, current year and for the first six months of the second year.

13. Sued by a competitor for alleged infringement of trade name. It is estimated that settlement could cost €50k.
14. A customer goes into liquidation, owing €6k to the company.
15. Interest of €3k is paid on the bank loan.

You should have a go at preparing the income statement, cash flow statement and closing balance sheet for Production Company for its first year of business. Once you have done this, you can compare your answer with the suggested solution given below.

Once you have completed the financial statements for Production Company's first year, you can have a go at the second year, for which the transactions and events are as follows.

1. Received €50k of inventory from suppliers, without having paid for it yet.
2. €80k of the inventory is sold for €205k, of which €50k is cash and €155k is on credit.
3. Interest of €3k is paid on the bank loan.
4. The bank loan is repaid in full.
5. Paid €30k in rent, for the period from the second half of the year.
6. The company decides to innovate and spends €35k on R&D.
7. The R&D is entirely unsuccessful.
8. It is discovered that the company's R&D efforts breached environmental legislation. The company expects to be fined approximately €20k. The fine remains unpaid at the year end.
9. Paid employees €25k.
10. The competitor company calls off its lawsuit. Trading Company is not required to make any payments.
11. Paid suppliers €20k.
12. Received €65k cash from customers.
13. Van depreciates to €12k.

Production Company suggested solution

The solution is presented in three parts. First, there is a written summary of the accounting treatment for each of the transactions and events. In each case, there is a balance sheet extract showing the effect of the double entry, in terms of the individual accounts, and the impact, if any, on the total for net assets/equity. Second, there is a summary of all of the journal entries. Third, there are the financial statements themselves. The accounting treatment for each of the transactions and events in the first year is as follows.

1. Purchasing a van involves the exchange of one asset (cash of €20k) for another (a van). We record the value of the van in the balance sheet at the amount that was paid for it. As one asset increases by €20k, while another decreases by €20k, there is no change in the total value of assets on the balance sheet, and so there is no profit or loss on the transaction, and the income statement is unaffected. The cash outflow of €20k is reported in the cash flow statement, and because the asset purchased has long-term value to the business, the payment is recorded as an investing cash flow.

	€k
Van	20
Cash	(20)
Net assets	0
Equity	0

2. The purchase of inventory again involves the exchange of one asset for another. The effect on the balance sheet is to increase inventory by €50k and reduce cash by €50k. The reduction in cash is classified as an operating cash flow in the cash flow statement, as the inventory will shortly be sold to customers and does not have long-term value to the business.

	€k
Inventory	50
Cash	(50)
Net assets	0
Equity	0

3. The effect of borrowing from the bank is that the business has a new asset (cash) and a new liability (bank loan). These changes to the balance sheet offset one another, and there is no overall change in the value of net assets; there is therefore neither a profit nor a loss. The total value of assets has increased, however, and so the business has become larger. As this growth has been financed by a bank loan, the percentage of the business now owned by the shareholders has reduced (they previously owned all of the business, whereas they now own only two-thirds). The inflow of cash is a capital injection from a provider of finance; it is therefore classified as a financing cash flow.

	€k
Cash	50
Bank loan	(50)
Net assets	**0**
Equity	**0**

4. Spending €15k on advertising reduces cash; this part of the transaction is objective and straightforward. Less obvious, however, is the treatment of the other half of the double entry. It could be argued that advertising is an investment: expenditure incurred with the aim of generating long-term benefits by means of higher future revenue. If this argument is accepted, then the advertising expenditure would be capitalised: the double entry would be a decrease in cash and an increase in intangible assets, with no overall effect on total assets or on profit or loss. The major difficulty with this argument, however, is that the value of advertising expenditure cannot be measured reliably. A further difficulty is that the benefits of advertising expenditure might, in any event, be short lived. In practice, therefore, advertising expenditure does not lead to the creation of an intangible asset but is instead treated as an expense: the double entry is to decrease both cash and profit. Correspondingly, the cash outflow is classified as operating in the cash flow statement.

	€k
Cash	(15)
Net assets	**(15)**
Retained profit	(15)
Equity	**(15)**

5. The payment of employees is treated in the same way as advertising. The reduction in cash is classified as an operating cash flow, and this amount is expensed rather than capitalised, so that no asset is created, the total value of net assets declines, and profit is reduced.

	€k
Cash	(25)
Net assets	**(25)**
Retained profit	(25)
Equity	**(25)**

6. The sale of inventory involves two separate transactions, occurring simultaneously. The first is the receipt of cash from the customer, for which the double entry is an increase in cash (an operating cash flow) and income (which is an increase in profit/equity). The second is the transfer of inventory from the business to the customer, for which the double entry is a decrease in inventory (a reduction in assets) and an expense (a reduction in profit/equity). The value of assets increases overall, because the increase of €125k in cash is greater than the reduction of €50k in inventory. Correspondingly, the value of equity also increases by €75k, which is equal to the income of €125k less the expense of €50k, as recorded in the income statement.

	€k
Inventory	(50)
Cash	125
Net assets	75
Retained profit	75
Equity	75

7. The increase in inventory of €80k is matched by an increase in accounts payable of €80k. There is no effect on the cash flow statement because the supplier has not yet been paid. Equally, there is no effect on the income statement, because there is no change in the overall value of net assets. The suppliers have in effect joined the shareholders and the bank as financiers of the business: in the same way that the business has more assets because the bank has provided finance, so the assets are also greater because the supplier has provided inventory, and both bank and supplier are liabilities of the business.

	€k
Inventory	80
Accounts payable	(80)
Net assets	0
Equity	0

8. The sale of inventory again involves two transactions. On this occasion, the sale is made on credit. The double entry for the sale is to increase income and increase accounts receivable.

The increase in assets has not yet come in the form of cash but instead in the form of accounts receivable, which measures the value of the company's right to receive cash from the customer. The double entry for the transfer of inventory is to reduce inventory and to reduce profit. Overall, net assets and equity both increase by €65k.

	€k
Inventory	(40)
Accounts receivable	105
Net assets	65
Retained profit	65
Equity	65

9. A payment to suppliers reduces cash (operating cash flow). If the payment is for inventory already received, then the other side of the double entry is to reduce accounts payable. The decrease in assets is therefore equal to the decrease in liabilities, meaning that the owners of the business are neither better nor worse off and there is no change in equity.

	€k
Cash	(20)
Accounts payable	20
Net assets	0
Equity	0

10. This example is the opposite of that of payments to suppliers. If the receipt from customers, which is an operating cash flow, is for sales already made, then the other side of the double entry is to reduce accounts receivable. The increase in one asset is equal to the decrease in another, meaning that there is no overall change in the value of assets or equity. There is, however, a change to the balance sheet, and the business is in somewhat better shape. Accounts receivable are unproductive assets, in contrast with cash, which can be invested to generate a return. There is also the possibility that customers may default, resulting in a write-off of accounts receivable, which makes it more desirable for assets to be in the form of cash rather than receivables.

	€k
Accounts receivable	(65)
Cash	65
Net assets	0
Equity	0

11. During the accounting period, the van has declined in value. Its estimated value in the balance sheet is now €16k, as opposed to the €20k for which it was purchased. Shareholders are worse off as a result of this decline. The double entry is a €4k reduction in fixed assets and a €4k expense. There is no effect on the cash flow statement.

	€k
Van	(4)
Net assets	(4)
Retained profit	(4)
Equity	(4)

12. The payment of rent reduces cash (operating cash flow). Normally, the other side of the double entry would simply be an expense, because the payment is for the use of a building and it does not create an asset. In this example, however, rent is paid for the whole of the current year and for six months of the following year. According to the principle of accruals accounting, only the expense incurred for renting the building during the accounting period should be included in the income statement. It does not matter whether the actual cash payment for rent was greater or less than the expense incurred. If the cash payment had been less than the rental expense, then it would have been necessary to create a liability on the balance sheet for the amount owed. In this case, however, the cash payment exceeds the expense, and so an asset is created on the balance sheet for the difference. If we assume that the annual rent is the same in each year, then the expense in the current year is €60k and the newly created asset (prepaid expenses) is €30k. Conceptually, the prepaid expense is an asset because it represents services that have been paid for but not yet received.

	€k
Prepaid expenses	30
Cash	(90)
Net assets	**(60)**
Retained profit	(60)
Equity	**(60)**

13. This example of being sued by a competitor introduces considerable subjectivity into the accounts. There is no simple answer, and a case could be made for one of a number of different accounting treatments. One possibility would be to do nothing. It could be argued that the competitor does not have a case, or alternatively that the estimated settlement is far too unreliable a number to be included in the financial statements. Another possibility would be to take a highly conservative approach. If settlement could cost €50k, then the double entry under this approach would be to create a liability (strictly, a provision) of €50k (which reduces net assets) and an expense of €50k (because the shareholders are worse off). In the solution given here, the Conservative approach is adopted. This should not be seen as necessarily the right answer but just as one possible answer. There is no effect on the cash flow statement. If, at some future date, the lawsuit is successful, then there would be a cash outflow. At the present date, however, there is a reduction in net assets, because shareholders are worse off facing a potential lawsuit then they would be otherwise, but there is no reduction in cash.

	€k
Provision	(50)
Net assets	**(50)**
Retained profit	(50)
Equity	**(50)**

14. If the customer going into liquidation means that the €6k that is owed will not be paid, then this requires a write-off of accounts receivable. The double entry is a reduction of €6k in accounts receivable and an expense of €6k resulting from this loss of assets. There is no effect on the cash flow statement. What has happened is that €6k of accounts receivable were originally recognised when sales were made, in the expectation that cash

Table 4.1 Journal entries for the first year

Reference	Account	Dr €k	Cr €k
1	Van	20	
	Cash (investing)		20
2	Inventory	50	
	Cash (operating)		50
3	Cash (financing)	50	
	Bank loan		50
4	Expense (advertising)	15	
	Cash (operating)		15
5	Expense (wages)	25	
	Cash (operating)		25
6	Cash (operating)	125	
	Income (sales)		125
	Expense (cost of sales)	50	
	Inventory		50
7	Inventory	80	
	Accounts payable		80
8	Accounts receivable	105	
	Income (sales)		105
	Expense (cost of sales)	40	
	Inventory		40
9	Accounts payable	20	
	Cash (operating)		20
10	Cash (operating)	65	
	Accounts receivable		65
11	Expense (depreciation)	4	
	Van		4
12	Expense (rent)	60	
	Prepaid expenses	30	
	Cash (operating)		90
13	Expense (lawsuit)	50	
	Provision		50

Table 4.1 (*cont.*)

Reference	Account	Dr €k	Cr €k
14	Expense (bad debt)	6	
	Accounts receivable		6
15	Expense (interest)	3	
	Cash (operating)		3

would ultimately be received. This expectation has now changed, and so an asset that was created without any associated cash flow has now disappeared, again without any associated cash flow.

	€k
Accounts receivable	(6)
Net assets	**(6)**
Retained profit	(6)
Equity	**(6)**

15. The final transaction in the first year is the payment of interest on a bank loan, for which the double entry is simply a reduction in cash and an expense. If the interest had not been paid in cash but was instead simply added to the value of the loan, then the double entry would have been an increase in the loan and an expense. Either way, by means of a reduction in cash or an increase in the liability, net assets decline, as a result of which shareholders are worse off and so there is an expense in the income statement.

	€k
Cash	(3)
Net assets	**(3)**
Retained profit	(3)
Equity	**(3)**

The journal entries for the first year are as shown in Table 4.1.

The financial statements for the first year are as shown in Table 4.2.

Table 4.2 Financial statements for the first year

Balance sheet for production company at the start of year 1	
	€k
Cash	100
	100
Share capital	100
	100

Income statement for production company for year 1	
	€k
Income	230
Cost of sales	(90)
Gross margin	140
Operating expenses	(160)
Profit before interest	(20)
Interest	(3)
Profit before tax	(23)
Tax	–
Profit after tax	(23)

Cash flow statement for production company for year 1	
	€k
Operating cash flow	(13)
Investing cash flow	(20)
Financing cash flow	50
Change in cash	17

Balance sheet for production company at the end of year 1	
	€k
Fixed assets	16
Inventory	40
Accounts receivable	34
Prepaid expenses	30
Cash	117
Assets	**237**
Bank loan	50
Provision	50
Accounts payable	60
Liabilities	**160**

Table 4.2 (cont.)

	€k
Net assets	77
Share capital	100
Retained profit	(23)
Equity	77

If you have successfully completed the financial statements for the first year, then those for the second year should be straightforward. In particular, you will notice repetition in the descriptions below relating to each transaction. This is because there are really not many options in the accounting treatment of any given transaction or event. Everything must affect the balance sheet in two places, and in each case must affect assets, liabilities or equity. If the asset of cash is affected, then the item is additionally reported in the cash flow statement and classified as either operating, investing or financing. If there is a gain or loss in equity, then the item is additionally reported either as income or expense in the income statement. That is all there is to it.

The accounting treatment for each of the items in the second year is as follows.

1. There is a €50k increase in assets (inventory) and a €50k increase in liabilities (accounts payable). Net assets do not change and so there is no effect on the income statement. There are no cash payments or receipts and so no effect on the cash flow statement.

	€k
Inventory	50
Accounts payable	(50)
Net assets	0
Equity	0

2. The double entry for the transfer of the inventory is €80k reduction in inventory and €80k expense. The double entry for the cash received from customers is a €50k increase in cash and €50k income, and for sales on credit, there is a €155k increase in accounts receivable and €155k income. Overall, net assets increase by €125k, which is equal to income of €205k less expenses of €80k.

	€k
Inventory	(80)
Accounts receivable	155
Cash	50
Net assets	125
Retained profit	125
Equity	125

3. The interest payment reduces cash and profit.

	€k
Cash	(3)
Net assets	(3)
Retained profit	(3)
Equity	(3)

4. The repayment of the bank loan reduces both assets and liabilities, with no overall effect on net assets. The double entry is a reduction in cash of €50k (classified as a financing cash flow because it is a repayment of capital) and a €50k reduction in the bank loan.

	€k
Cash	(50)
Bank loan	50
Net Assets	0
Equity	0

5. The payment of rent for the reporting period is simply a reduction in cash and an expense. A complication, however, is that the reporting period started with a prepaid expense opening balance, representing the cost of rent for the first six months of the period. This asset is consumed during that six-month period and so it should be removed from the closing balance sheet. The appropriate double entry is a reduction in the asset of €30k and expense of €30k. Overall, the effect of these two double entries is that a rental expense included in the income statement for the year is €60k.

	€k
Prepaid expenses	(30)
Cash	(30)
Net assets	(60)
Retained profit	(60)
Equity	(60)

6. The investment of €35k in R&D is presumably made with a view to long-term economic benefit. Conceptually, it would therefore be appropriate to capitalise this expenditure. As the economic value of R&D cannot be measured reliably, however, the accounting treatment in practice would be to expense the €35k. The double entry is therefore a reduction of €35k in cash and an expense of €35k.

	€k
Cash	(35)
Net assets	(35)
Retained profit	(35)
Equity	(35)

7. The R&D proves to be unsuccessful. From an accounting perspective, this does not matter, because the R&D has already been expensed. There is no R&D asset in the accounts and therefore nothing to be written off now that the R&D has proven to be unsuccessful. There is no need to do anything.

8. This example is similar to the lawsuit in the previous year, except that the amount payable and the likelihood that it will be paid are probably both more certain. The correct accounting treatment is to create a liability for the amount that the company expects to pay. The double entry is an increase in provisions of €20k and an expense of €20k. The fact that the fine remains unpaid at the end of the year simply means that there is no effect on the cash flow statement and that there is a liability in the closing balance sheet.

	€k
Provision	(20)
Net assets	(20)
Retained profit	(20)
Equity	(20)

9. The double entry for wages or salaries is a reduction in cash and an expense.

	€k
Cash	(25)
Net assets	**(25)**
Retained profit	(25)
Equity	**(25)**

10. If the competitor called off the lawsuit, then any liability that has been recognised is no longer required and must be removed. The double entry is a reduction in liabilities and an increase in equity. There is no effect on the cash flow statement, and the asset of cash was affected neither when the liability was recognised nor when it was derecognised. In contrast, the income statement reported an expense last year on recognition of the liability, while it reports the opposite in the current year as the liability is taken away. In other words, profit is higher by €50k in the second year as a result of creating a liability in the first year that proved to be unfounded.

	€k
Provision	50
Net assets	**50**
Retained profit	50
Equity	**50**

11. The payment to suppliers reduces both cash and accounts payable.

	€k
Cash	(20)
Accounts payable	20
Net assets	**0**
Equity	**0**

12. The receipt from customers increases cash and reduces accounts receivable.

Table 4.3 Journal entries for the second year

Reference	Account	Dr €k	Cr €k
1	Inventory	50	
	Accounts payable		50
2	Cash (operating)	50	
	Income (sales)		50
	Accounts receivable	155	
	Income (sales)		155
	Expense (cost of sales)	80	
	Inventory		80
3	Expense (interest)	3	
	Cash (operating)		3
4	Bank loan	50	
	Cash (financing)		50
5	Expense (rent)	30	
	Cash (operating)		30
	Expense (rent)	30	
	Prepaid expenses		30
6	Expense (R&D)	35	
	Cash (operating)		35
8	Expense (fines)	20	
	Provision		20
9	Expense (wages)	25	
	Cash (operating)		25
10	Provision	50	
	Expense (lawsuit)		50
11	Accounts payable	20	
	Cash (operating)		20
12	Cash (operating)	65	
	Accounts receivable		65
13	Expense (depreciation)	4	
	Van		4

Table 4.4 Financial statements for the second year

Income statement for production company for year 2	
	€k
Income	205
Cost of sales	(80)
Gross margin	125
Operating expenses	(94)
Profit before interest	(31)
Interest	(3)
Profit before tax	28
Tax	–
Profit after tax	28
Cash flow statement for production company for year 2	
	€k
Operating cash flow	2
Investing cash flow	–
Financing cash flow	(50)
Change in cash	(48)
Balance sheet for production company at the end of year 2	
	€k
Fixed assets	12
Inventory	10
Accounts receivable	124
Prepaid expenses	–
Cash	69
Assets	**215**
Bank loan	–
Provision	20
Accounts payable	90
Liabilities	**110**
Net assets	**105**
Share capital	100
Retained profit	5
Equity	**105**

	€k
Accounts receivable	(65)
Cash	65
Net assets	0
Equity	0

13. The double entry for depreciation is a €4k reduction in fixed assets and a €4k expense. There is no effect on the cash flow statement.

	€k
Van	(4)
Net assets	**(4)**
Retained profit	(4)
Equity	**(4)**

The journal entries for the second year are as shown in Table 4.3.

The financial statements for the second year are as shown in Table 4.4.

Part II

Part I of the book comprised an overview of the foundations of accounting, including the purpose of financial statements, the process by which financial transactions and events are recorded in the accounting system, and the ways in which accounting information is presented.

In Part II, the focus now shifts to the use of the financial statements, with an emphasis on how accounting information can deepen understanding of business performance. While Part II introduces significant new material, it will also draw heavily upon Part I, so that you will have considerable opportunity to consolidate the material that we have covered so far.

The content of Part II is structured as follows.

Chapter 5: The accounts as a lens on growth Chapter 5 explores how the financial statements, and in particular the cash flow statement and the balance sheet, can be used to understand the rate of growth that the organisation has achieved, as well as the routes by which the growth has taken place.

Chapter 6: Measuring value creation Chapter 6 evaluates how accounting data can be used to evaluate economic performance, as measured primarily by the return earned by a company on its shareholders' capital. Specifically, a company can increase its return on capital if, first, it increases its efficiency in employing assets to generate sales revenue and, second, it increases the profit margins earned on those sales. Chapter 6 also introduces the concept of economic profit, which is a measure that compares the return on capital earned by a company with that available to investors in alternative investments.

Chapter 7: Understanding risk Any organisation is exposed to a variety of risks, some of which are financial in nature and can be evident from the financial statements. Chapter 7 identifies and discusses two such sources of risk, both of which are related to the concept of leverage (or gearing). Specifically, an organisation has high operating leverage if its fixed costs are high in relation to its variable costs, and high financial leverage if its capital structure comprises a high level of debt in relation to equity. Higher leverage is associated with higher risk, as measured by returns to shareholders.

Chapter 8: Building a corporate valuation model   While the first seven chapters of the book have focused primarily on what might be termed the historical role of financial statements, namely the recording of past financial performance, there is also an important forward-looking role for financial statement data. This is illustrated in Chapter 8, which brings together much of the material from previous chapters to build a model which forecasts financial statement data and determines a company valuation.

5 | The accounts as a lens on growth

The accounts as a lens on growth

Part Two of this book will review several applications of accounting information. We will start by examining how the accounts shed light on the evolution of a business over time, in particular what the factors are that enable the business to grow.

A first observation is that a business can achieve growth in its assets in either of two ways. First, it can use its existing assets to generate further assets. This is what happens when, for example, inventory is sold for an amount greater than cost: the loss of one asset (inventory) is exceeded by the gain in another asset (accounts receivable or cash). A business might also have invested in financial securities that generate a regular interest income, in which case assets grow as that income is received. Assets might also be used indirectly to generate further assets, for example where equipment is used in the development of a product or service, which leads ultimately to sales being made to customers and to cash being received. In general, for each of these cases and more, the profitable employment of assets leads to growth in assets. This is a familiar conclusion. In Part I, we saw that profit results from growth in net assets, and so achieving growth by using existing assets to generate further assets is really just another way of describing making a profit.

The second way to increase assets is through external funding, for example from shareholders or from the bank. If a company issues new shares, then its cash balance will increase. This cash can in turn be invested in the business, for example to acquire new equipment or inventory, or even to make acquisitions of other businesses. Similarly, raising a new loan from the bank also increases assets.

The financial statements tell the story of a company's growth. Whether a company makes profits and reinvests these to create growth, or whether it borrows in order to fund the acquisition of assets, it leaves behind a trail of transactions that are recorded in the accounts. As this chapter will show, reading the accounts is akin to reading the story of the company's growth.

We will start by looking at what the cash flow statement has to say about growth. The next step will be to consider the effects of cash flows on the balance sheet, followed by consideration of the impact of accruals and of the information contained in the income statement.

Cash flow statement

A simple reading of the cash flow statement provides an insight into whether a company is growing and, if so, by what means. A simple illustration of this is provided in Table 5.1, which reports summary cash flow statements for nine companies, which are named Company A through to Company I. In each case, there is no overall change in the amount of cash held by the company during the reporting period. Yet each cash flow statement tells a different story. Before reading the next paragraph, take a look at Table 5.1 and see if you can determine, for each company, whether there is growth in assets and, if so, by what means the growth is being achieved. To do this, you should draw upon your understanding from Part I of the categories of the cash flow statement.

Operating cash flow is a measure of the difference between cash received from customers and cash paid out to run the business, for example to pay suppliers and employees. It follows that if a company reports positive operating cash flow, then it is generating a cash surplus from its trading activities. Other things being equal, this will lead to an increase in assets.

Companies A, B and C are all in this position of generating a positive operating cash flow, and moreover each generates the same amount. Each company differs, however, in their investing and financing cash flows.

Investing cash flow is a measure of the value of long-lived assets acquired or disposed of. If a company reports a negative investing cash flow, then it is using cash to acquire assets. While this does not lead to a change in the total value of assets, there is an increase in assets dedicated to the business purpose of the organisation, for example more buildings or equipment. A positive cash flow, on the other hand, implies the disposal of assets, and therefore shrinkage in the productive capacity of the business.

Table 5.1 Nine different routes to zero net cash flow

	A €k	B €k	C €k	D €k	E €k	F €k	G €k	H €k	I €k
Operating cash flow	10	10	10	0	−10	−10	−10	0	0
Investing cash flow	−10	0	10	−10	−10	0	10	10	0
Financing cash flow	0	−10	−20	10	20	10	0	−10	0
Change in cash	0	0	0	0	0	0	0	0	0

Company A has generated operating cash flow of €10k, all of which is reinvested in the business to acquire new assets. While there is no net increase in Company A's cash balance, the total value of its assets has grown. Moreover, it has achieved this growth without the benefit of additional funding from shareholders or from the bank. It is a successful business that is growing organically. The company could, of course, have grown even more if it had decided to also raise funds externally. A bank loan of €15k, for example, would have enabled overall growth in assets of €25k. The company is perhaps being conservative, because it is restricting its capacity to grow by using only internal funding.

Company B has also generated operating cash flow of €10k, but in contrast with Company A, it has not reinvested this amount in the business but has instead returned it to providers of finance. In other words, it has either paid dividends, repurchased shares or paid off bank loans. As a consequence, the total assets of Company B have not grown: all the surplus that was generated internally by the business during the reporting period was transferred out of the business and back into the pockets of shareholders or the bank. While Company B has traded just as successfully as Company A, it differs because it is a no-growth company.

Company C, meanwhile, is scaling down its activities even though it, too, has positive operating cash flow. Instead of reinvesting in the business, it has actually sold long-lived assets, resulting in a positive investing cash flow. The total of operating plus investing cash flow has been returned to providers of finance, who have withdrawn more assets out of the company during the period than the company has been able to generate. The business is possibly near the end of its life cycle, and while it is still making money, it no longer has opportunities for profitable investments, such that providers of finance are now withdrawing their money in order to reinvest elsewhere.

Company D has grown at the same rate as Company A, yet it differs in that the source of funding for its growth has been external rather than internal (a financing cash flow rather than an operating cash flow). This is perhaps a young business that has not yet been able to generate positive operating cash flow, yet which is investing in long-lived assets because it expects them to generate trading surpluses in the future.

Company E might also be a young business, which is incurring both operating and investing cash outflows as it seeks to establish and develop its business. The company has no option but to borrow heavily in order to be able to cover these cash outflows. Company E has grown at the same rate as Companies A and D but it has only been able to do so by borrowing more heavily. Investors and management will be watching future operating cash flows carefully, because these must become positive for the business to be sustainable.

Company F has the same negative operating cash flow as Company E, yet its position is perhaps more worrying. The company has had to raise funds externally in order to cover the cash outflows from its trading activities. If this borrowing was from the bank, then it now has a new loan to repay and interest costs to cover, yet it has no net increase in its assets, because the cash received from the bank was cancelled out by the loss of cash from trading activities. There has been no investing cash flow, suggesting that, unlike Companies D and E, the company does not have profitable investment opportunities available to it, but instead has to look for a turnaround in trading conditions for its operating cash flow to improve and for the business to be sustainable.

Company G appears to be in a somewhat similar position to Company F. Both have a negative operating cash flow, and neither is growing. While Company F has funded its operations by raising finance externally, however, Company G has pursued the alternative option of selling off some of its assets. This is symptomatic of a business in trouble. It might, for example, have been forced to sell assets because shareholders and the banks were unwilling to invest any more money in the business. It might also have raised as much as it could from asset sales by selling off some of the better-performing parts of its business. If so, it will no longer benefit from the cash flows that those businesses generate, and the one-off cash inflow from asset disposals will be offset in future years by even worse operating cash flows. On the other hand, it is possible that Company G owned assets that it was not using effectively but that were valuable to others in the industry,

Table 5.2 A summary of the nine different routes to zero net cash flow

		Operating cash flow		
		Positive	Nil	Negative
Growth	**Positive**	A	D	E
	Nil	B	I	F
	Negative	C	H	G

in which case the company's position would not be so bad. Either way, however, the combination of negative operating cash flows and positive investing cash flows suggests the restructuring of a troubled business.

Company H, meanwhile, is also disposing of assets, yet by doing so it is returning money to its providers of finance. This suggests a lack of profitable investment opportunities and a winding down of the business. There does not, however, appear to be any particular cause for concern; while operating cash flow may not be positive, neither is it negative.

Each of the scenarios in Table 5.1 is summarised in Table 5.2 including, for completeness, the simplest case, Company I, where the net cash flow is zero in all categories. Table 5.2 summarises the two main themes of the discussion above. The first is whether there is growth in assets, in other words whether investing cash flows are zero. The second is the means by which growth is achieved, in other words whether internally, by means of operating cash flow, or externally, by means of financing cash flow.

As you know from Part I, each of the transactions reported in the cash flow statement is one part of a double entry, with the other part affecting some other account on the balance sheet. With operating cash flow, the other account is retained profit, which is a component of equity. With investing cash flow, the other account is an asset of some kind, such as land, buildings or equipment. With financing cash flow, the other account relates to a provider of finance, notably bank loans or equity (shareholders' funds). Having reviewed the cash flows, we will now review the other side of the double entry to which the cash flows relate.

Balance sheet

Table 5.3 presents balance sheets for each of the nine companies discussed above. Table 5.3 first reports an opening balance sheet that is common to all companies, and then it updates this balance sheet

Table 5.3 Balance sheets for the nine companies

	Opening €k	A €k	B €k	C €k	D €k	E €k	F €k	G €k	H €k	I €k
Fixed assets	100	110	100	90	110	110	100	90	90	100
Accounts receivable	40	40	40	40	40	40	40	40	40	40
Cash	30	30	30	30	30	30	30	30	30	30
Total assets	170	180	170	160	180	180	170	160	160	170
Bank loan	45	45	35	25	55	65	55	45	35	45
Accounts payable	5	5	5	5	5	5	5	5	5	5
Total liabilities	50	50	40	30	60	70	60	50	40	50
Equity	120	130	130	130	120	110	110	110	120	120

for each of the cash flow statements from Table 5.1 (it is assumed that there are no other transactions other than these cash flows).

Before looking in detail at Table 5.3, you should have a go at preparing it for yourself. Taking the opening balance sheet from Table 5.3 and the cash flows from Table 5.1, create closing balance sheets for each of the nine companies, and then compare your answers with those in Table 5.3. For information, it is assumed in Table 5.3 that the financing cash flows affect the size of the bank loan and do not have any effect on equity.

It is obvious from looking at the balance sheets which companies have grown their total assets and which have not. Moreover, you will have noticed that the increase in total assets is determined by the level of investing cash flow. This is because there was no net change in inventory, accounts receivable or cash, and increases in fixed assets arise from capital expenditure (i.e. investing cash flow). Companies A, D and E each invested €10k and total assets grew by €10k, while Companies B, F and I did not invest, and Companies C, G and H disposed of assets.

Total liabilities, meanwhile, increased by an amount equal to financing cash flow. This is because there was no net change in accounts payable, and increases in the bank loan arise from new borrowing (i.e. financing cash flow). Companies D, E and F each borrowed during the reporting period, while Companies B, C and H each paid down part of their outstanding bank loan.

The final category on the balance sheet, equity, increased by an amount equal to the operating cash flow. If the financing cash flows had been between the company and its shareholders as opposed to being between the company and its bank, then these would also have affected the equity balance. If there had been accruals in addition to operating cash flows, for example if there had been an increase in accounts receivable resulting from sales made on credit, then this, too, would have affected the equity balance. In this simple example, however, the only double entry to affect equity results from operating cash flow which changes the cash and equity accounts on the balance sheet. In other words, profit is equal to operating cash flow in this example.

So far, so good, but what happens if we introduce some additional real-world complexity to the example? Specifically, what happens if the fixed assets depreciate? And what happens if there are changes in working capital, caused by a change in accounts receivable, or accounts payable? How would each of these affect growth?

Suppose that the fixed asset depreciates by €7k during the reporting period. This has no effect on the cash flow statement but for all companies profit will now be €7k less than operating cash flow and the book value of fixed assets will also be lower by €7k. The growth in assets is now equal to the value of capital expenditure (investing cash flow) less the amount of depreciation. In other words, each company is required to undertake capital expenditure in order simply to maintain the productive capacity of the business, and only further expenditure above this level will enable the business to grow. With the introduction of depreciation, only three of our nine companies (A, D and E) will now have grown during the reporting period, and even then only by an increase in assets of €3k, while the total assets of all other companies will have reduced.

The ratio of capital expenditure to depreciation can be used as an indicator of growth. If the ratio exceeds one, the company is making sufficient investment in the business to enable fixed assets to grow. If the ratio falls short of one, on the other hand, then the level of investment in new assets is insufficient to keep up with the depreciation of existing assets.

While depreciation does not itself involve cash flow, it does have cash implications for a company. If assets depreciate, and if the company wishes to replace them in order to maintain productive capacity, then it must increase investing cash outflows, which in turn implies that it must find cash from somewhere, either by reinvesting a greater amount of its operating cash flow, by using its existing cash balance or by increasing financing cash inflows. Among our nine companies, none of A, D, E, F, G, H or I is able to increase investing cash outflows from operating cash flow generated during the period, either because all of the operating cash flow is already being reinvested (Company A) or because positive operating cash flow is not being generated in the first place. In all of these cases, an increase in investing cash flow would require either a financing cash inflow or the use of some of the cash that is sitting on the company's balance sheet. In contrast, Companies B and C have both generated positive operating cash flow but they have not reinvested this in the business, and so for these companies there remains the possibility of the internally generated funding of capital expenditure.

Now suppose that, in addition to depreciation, there is also an increase in accounts receivable and accounts payable. What effect do these increases have on growth?

An increase in accounts receivable implies that income has been recognised in the income statement but cash has not yet been received. For each of our nine companies, operating cash flow therefore understates trading performance, because the gains from trade are in part captured by the increase in accounts receivable. In contrast, an increase in accounts payable can be viewed as the opposite of an increase in accounts receivable. An increase in accounts payable implies the recognition of expenses in the income statement which have not yet been paid for, meaning that the outflows captured in operating cash flow understate the expenses incurred by the business.

If we suppose that the increase in accounts receivable for each company was 9 and the increase in accounts payable was €3k, and if we also account for the depreciation of €7k, then how would the balance sheets for each of the companies differ from those in Table 5.3? The answer is given in Table 5.4, but before looking at this you should have a go at preparing the answer for yourself, by taking the balance sheet for each of the companies and updating them for the double entries involving depreciation, accounts receivable and accounts payable.

Take a look at Table 5.4, compare it with your own answer and make sure that you can follow how the discussion above corresponds to each balance sheet, in terms of the effects of

Table 5.4 Balance sheets with depreciation and increase in accounts receivable

	Opening €k	A €k	B €k	C €k	D €k	E €k	F €k	G €k	H €k	I €k
Fixed assets	100	103	93	83	103	103	93	83	83	93
Accounts receivable	40	49	49	49	49	49	49	49	49	49
Cash	30	30	30	30	30	30	30	30	30	30
Total assets	170	182	172	162	182	182	172	162	162	172
Bank loan	45	45	35	25	55	65	55	45	35	45
Accounts payable	5	8	8	8	8	8	8	8	8	8
Total liabilities	50	53	43	33	63	73	63	53	43	53
Equity	120	129	129	129	119	109	109	109	119	119

depreciation, accounts receivable and accounts payable in making the data in Table 5.4 different from those in Table 5.3.

Income statement

As we have seen, with depreciation, and changes to accounts receivable and accounts payable, there are changes to the book value of net assets that are not the consequence of cash flows. There is therefore not a complete story of growth provided by the cash flow statement alone. To illustrate this, have a go at creating the income statements for each of the companies. For this purpose, assume that the cash outflows for operating expenses were €30k for each company, and the cash inflows from customers were €40k for Companies A, B and C, €30k for D, H and I, and €20k for E, F and G. Once you have completed the income statements, compare your answer with that in Table 5.5.

Overall, profit is equal to the change in net assets, and it is therefore a measure of growth. There remain, however, reasons to find other statements useful also. To illustrate, consider accounts receivable. Even though income is recognised whether or not cash has actually been received, it is always preferable to hold assets in the form of cash rather than accounts receivable, because cash can

Table 5.5 Income statements

	A €k	B €k	C €k	D €k	E €k	F €k	G €k	H €k	I €k
Income	49	49	49	39	29	29	29	39	39
Expenses	–33	–33	–33	–33	–33	–33	–33	–33	–33
Depreciation	–7	–7	–7	–7	–7	–7	–7	–7	–7
Profit	**9**	**9**	**9**	**–1**	**–11**	**–11**	**–11**	**–1**	**–1**

be reinvested in the business, while receivables are unproductive assets and subject to the risk of customer default. Further, if you compare Company A with Company C, you will see that both have the same profit, but the balance sheets of each have changed differently, and with different implications for productive capacity and so for the future growth of the company. Specifically, Company A has reinvested operating cash flow into fixed assets, while Company C has divested fixed assets and used the cash from this and from operating activities to repay bank loans. Each company ends up with the same amount of net assets, but Company A has the larger business (more assets and also more liabilities).

In summary

As we have seen, the financial statements capture the trail left by a company's growth. The cash flow statement reports the investing cash flows made to expand the business, as well as identifying whether those cash flows have been funded internally, from operating activity, or externally, from financing activity. The opening and closing balance sheets report how each of the company's assets and liabilities have increased during the period, whether as a result of cash flows or of accruals, such as depreciation. The income statement reports the overall growth in equity resulting from profitable trading activity, whether or not there is a corresponding change in cash.

While the financial statements can provide useful information and insight, there will always, however, be questions that remain unanswered. Consider, for example, the lack of information inherent in each of the following, where a reading of the financial statements can help to identify issues that need to be explored but where the financial statements themselves cannot provide unambiguous answers.

- The book value of fixed assets increases if capital expenditure exceeds depreciation. It is reasonable to suppose that a company's productive capacity also increases in this situation. This need not necessarily be the case, however, and in general a given percentage increase in fixed assets need not equate to the same percentage increase in productive capacity. There are several reasons for this. If, for example, an asset has the same productive capacity throughout its life, then even though the value of the asset declines with depreciation, the productive capacity does not; capacity does not decline gradually, as represented by the annual depreciation expense, but instead disappears abruptly and altogether when the asset reaches the end of its life. An alternative scenario is that depreciation relates to installed assets of one type, while capital expenditure relates to a new type of asset altogether, representing a different technology with a different productive capacity, or perhaps even relating to an entirely different product or service. In such a case, a like-for-like comparison between capital expenditure and depreciation cannot be made. In general, the change in fixed assets recorded in the accounts is only a high level, potentially ambiguous summary of a complex combination of underlying changes.
- Many businesses do not have a significant investment in fixed assets, and for such companies and many others, the value of fixed assets on the balance sheet may not be a good proxy for productive capacity. A services business, for example, is by nature less fixed asset intensive than a manufacturing business. Any company may lease its assets rather than own them, with the effect that fixed assets are employed in the business but need not show up on the balance sheet. Also, a company may make significant investments that increase its capacity to generate revenue, but it may be unable to capitalise these, meaning that they are reported as operating cash outflows and expensed, rather than as investing cash flows, and so as fixed assets on the balance sheet. The obvious examples are R&D and investment in the company's brand. For companies such as these, the income statement provides better information than the balance sheet on investing for growth.

- The financial statements can provide evidence of decisions made by management, for example capital expenditure that has been undertaken, or amounts that have been borrowed from the bank or raised from shareholders. There is limited evidence, however, on the effectiveness of those decisions. Capital expenditure is recorded at whatever it cost to undertake, not at the value it might be expected to generate. The capital expenditure decision might have been a great one, or it might prove to be a disaster. At the time that the decision is made, the financial statements are silent on the likely success of the project, and information on this must be sought elsewhere. This is a theme that we will return to in Chapters 6 and 8.

In general, the financial statements provide only part of the story. They capture the financial consequences of decisions, so enabling the reader to analyse the growth of the company, but they probably also prompt more questions than answers. This theme will be picked up again in the next chapter, which concerns the analysis of value creation.

6 | Measuring value creation

Measuring value creation

The previous chapter discussed how the financial statements can shed light on the growth of a business. It was shown that growth can come from either of two sources: reinvested profit or external funding. An important connection remains to be made, however, between growth and the creation of wealth, or value. As we shall see, growth is not necessarily a good thing. While we have established that a company becomes bigger by investing in additional assets, the issue we have yet to consider is whether this investment can be regarded as effective, in the sense that it creates value. Measuring value creation is therefore the subject of this chapter. We will start by making a distinction between the cost of making an investment and the return that is earned on that investment. We will then explore various factors that contribute to the return on investment.

Investment, growth and return on capital

When a company makes an investment in assets, it expects those assets to generate a return, and the effectiveness of the investment can be measured by the size of the return. It follows that if growth is measured by the investment in new assets, then it is not really a measure of performance. It is a measure of the cost of making an investment, and not of the return that the investment generates; an investment *of* capital, rather than a return *on* capital.

To illustrate, imagine a portfolio of shares that you own and manage. The portfolio will grow by €500 if you take €500 out of your bank account and buy some new shares. In this case, the growth is clearly the result of making a new investment and it is not a measure of return on investment (i.e. of performance). Suppose, however, that share prices now increase, which causes growth of €100 in the value of your portfolio. In this case, growth and return on investment are one and the same; they are both different ways to describe the profit that you have made. You can now choose whether to retain the profit within your portfolio, which is equivalent to a company reinvesting profit, or whether to sell €100 of shares, leaving the €500 that you invested originally, which is equivalent to a company paying a dividend.

If you decide the former, and reinvest your profits, then you are in effect making a new investment: by choosing not to withdraw your funds, you are by default investing them. A decision to grow is therefore a decision to invest. You may expect a different return from your investment if, in the past, instead of having earned a profit of €100 on an initial investment of €500, you had instead earned €200 on an initial investment of €400, or indeed if you were making a new investment of €600. In each case, however, you are currently making the same economic decision to invest €600, and whatever the source of this investment, this €600 is a measure of the capital that you are putting in, not of the return that you are getting out.

As an investor, your primary concern is with the relationship between how much you put in and how much you get out. Capital employed is a measure of the former, and profit of the latter, and it is the relationship between these two measures that matters. If a large profit was made, while there was only a small investment of capital, then the investment was particularly successful, and vice versa. In other words, our concern is with the rate of return: the profit that we make as a percentage of the capital that was invested. This stands to reason. The performance of an investment portfolio is not measured in absolute terms, but as a percentage gain on the investment that was made. Likewise, the interest earned on a bank account is expressed as a percentage rate of return. Neither growth in capital employed nor profit alone is a sufficient measure of performance; we need both.

The accounts provide measures of both the capital employed in a business and the profit that is earned on that capital, making it straightforward to determine a percentage rate of return. If the capital invested in a company was, say, €500, and if the profit earned was €30, then the return on this capital is 6 per cent.

$$\text{Return on invested capital (ROIC)} = \frac{\text{Profit}}{\text{Invested Capital}}$$

As we will see later on, there are alternative definitions of return on capital, depending upon the source from which the capital is raised. In particular, the return on equity (ROE) measures the return on shareholders' capital, while the return on capital employed (ROCE) measures the return on the combined capital provided by shareholders and debtholders. At this stage, we are using ROIC as an entirely general measure of return on capital; ROE and ROCE are more precisely defined versions of ROIC, and they will be introduced later.

The relationship between growth, profit and capital employed is illustrated in Table 6.1, which contrasts a company that is profitable but does not grow (Company A), with a profitable, growth company (Company B) with an unprofitable company that grows by means of external funding (Company C). These examples are simplified by assuming that there are no accruals, such that there is no difference between profit and operating cash flow (i.e. assets do not depreciate, and there is no change in working capital). Before reading on, take a look at Table 6.1 and try to make sense of everything that is going on. This is a useful exercise, because Table 6.1 not only illustrates the discussion above, but it is also an opportunity to reinforce your understanding of the relationships among the financial statements.

Company A is profitable but it does not grow. During year 1, its assets generate a profit of €100k, which is a return on invested capital of 10 per cent. All of this profit is realised during the year, such that operating cash flow is also €100k. The company decides not to reinvest this cash flow, but instead to pay all of it as a dividend to shareholders. The financing cash flow is therefore equal and opposite to the operating cash flow, there is no investing cash flow, and there is no increase in retained profit, because the profit earned during the period is exactly offset by the dividend paid. This pattern is repeated in years 2 and 3. Overall, Company A is profitable and generates a 10 per cent return on shareholders' investment every year, but the company does not grow, in sales, profit or assets.

Company B achieves the same ROIC as company A, but it differs in that it reinvests the profit in order to grow the business. Instead of returning cash to shareholders, the Company acquires new assets. The effect, in contrast with company A, is that assets increase and retained profit increases. In year 2, Company B again achieves the same ROIC as Company A, but because it starts the year with greater capital, so it makes greater profit. As in the previous year, this amount is reinvested, and so, by again earning a 10 per cent return, sales, profit and assets all become greater still by the end of year 2, and greater again by the end of year 3.

Company C achieves the same level of growth as Company B, yet it does so by raising new share capital, rather than by making and

Table 6.1 Profitability and growth

	Company A				Company B				Company C			
	Opening Balance €k	End of Year 1 €k	End of Year 2 €k	End of Year 3 €k	Opening Balance €k	End of Year 1 €k	End of Year 2 €k	End of Year 3 €k	Opening Balance €k	End of Year 1 €k	End of Year 2 €k	End of Year 3 €k
Balance sheet												
Assets	1,000	1,000	1,000	1,000	1,000	1,100	1,210	1,331	1,000	1,100	1,210	1,331
Share capital	1,000	1,000	1,000	1,000	1,000	1,000	1,000	1,000	1,000	1,100	1,210	1,331
Retained profit	0	0	0	0	0	100	210	331	0	0	0	0
Equity	1,000	1,000	1,000	1,000	1,000	1,100	1,210	1,331	1,000	1,100	1,210	1,331
Income statement												
Sales		500	500	500		500	550	605		500	550	605
Expenses		−400	−400	−400		−400	−440	−484		−500	−550	−605
Profit		100	100	100		100	110	121		0	0	0
Cash flow statement												
Operating		100	100	100		100	110	121		0	0	0
Investing		0	0	0		−100	−110	−121		−100	−110	−121
Financing		−100	−100	−100		0	0	0		100	110	121
Change in cash		0	0	0		0	0	0		0	0	0
ROIC		10%	10%	10%		10%	10%	10%		0%	0%	0%

reinvesting profits. In fact, Company C makes no profit at all: its ROIC is O per cent. In contrast with Company B, the growth in equity is in the form of new share capital rather than retained profit, and in contrast with Company A, its financing cash flow is positive rather than negative.

It is only in the case of Company B, therefore, that growth and profitability go hand in hand. In contrast, Company A is profitable but, because it has not reinvested, it has not grown, while Company C has grown in spite of being unprofitable, which has been possible by raising additional share capital.

While it is Companies B and C that have grown, it is Companies A and B that are more attractive from an investor's perspective, because they are profitable. Moreover, even though Company B has grown while Company A has not, they are equally attractive to investors, as both have provided a 10 per cent return on invested capital.

Evaluating the return on capital

The discussion so far has shown the importance of the ROIC, as a measure that captures both the profit that the company earns and the amount of capital that is employed to generate that profit. We can extend this discussion further by showing how a whole range of financial metrics can be linked back to the ROIC, enabling a greater understanding of the components that make up an entity's overall return on capital.

The critical first step is to recognise that the ROIC can be viewed as the product of two component parts, as follows.

$$\text{Return on invested capital (ROIC)} = \frac{\text{Profit}}{\text{Revenue}} \times \frac{\text{Revenue}}{\text{Invested capital}}$$

i.e.

$$\text{Return on invested capital (ROIC)} = \text{Profit margin} \times \text{Asset turnover}$$

In other words, the return on invested capital is the product of the profitability of sales (profit margin) and the efficiency with which assets are used (asset turnover). The underlying logic is that investors' capital is used to buy assets, with which the organisation generates output, which, net of expenses, generates profit. In order, therefore, to better understand the drivers of ROIC, it is necessary to examine the output generated in relation to the assets employed (asset turnover) and other costs incurred in making a profit out of sales (profit margin). This can all be illustrated by taking the example of a retail company.

The profit margin for a retailer depends in part upon the gross margin, which in turn depends upon the difference between the prices that it can charge its customers and the prices that it pays to its suppliers. The profit margin also depends upon the level of other operating expenses, such as costs of employment, advertising, depreciation of buildings and equipment, and so on. These costs are often reported as a percentage of sales, which provides a metric that is comparable over time and that can be benchmarked against other organisations. The specific costs that are identified in this way will vary, of course, across different industries, and there are no fixed rules concerning which costs to analyse. Moreover, the interpretation of a cost/sales ratio will differ significantly depending upon the specific cost under consideration. In particular costs such as R&D, advertising, product development or training might be viewed more as investments intended to generate future profits, in contrast with other costs that are viewed purely as expenses of the period. A reduction in the first of these categories of cost would improve the current profit margin, although most likely at the expense of future sales growth and/or future profit margin. A reduction in the second category, on the other hand, is more likely to be viewed as unambiguously positive, improving the current profit margin and enhancing the prospect of higher future profit margins.

All of the items affecting the profit margin are reported, of course, in the income statement. In order to maximise control over the ROIC, however, the retailer also needs to pay attention to its balance sheet, in order to maximise asset turnover. This can be illustrated using three specific cases of assets held by a retailer: retail stores, inventory and accounts receivable.

Retailers are concerned not just with the level of sales that they generate, but instead with sales per square metre of retail space. While it is always possible to increase sales simply by increasing capital employed, the same is not true for sales per square metre. By linking sales to retail space in this way, there is therefore explicit recognition of asset utilisation. Managers can compare sales per square metre across stores, or even across different areas within the same store, to determine the relative efficiency of capital employed. Taking the argument one step further, if retail space is more expensive to acquire in one location rather than another – say in the city centre, rather than out of town – then the ratio of sales to cost per square metre can be used to compare stores, because it takes into account differences in both the efficiency of asset utilisation and the cost of the asset.

A second important asset for a retailer is inventory. If a retailer can reduce its level of inventory, without adversely affecting sales, it will increase its ROIC. In part, this may result from an improvement in profit margin, because lower inventory levels may reduce operating expenses incurred by holding inventory, such as storage costs, insurance, obsolescence, and so on. Whether or not margins improve, however, capital employed will certainly be lower, and so ROIC higher.

In order to make sense of whether a given level of inventory is high or low, it is possible to make a connection between the balance sheet and the income statement, in the form of a ratio termed inventory turnover. Specifically, if the cost of sales measures the amount of inventory that is sold during the course of a financial year, then this can be used to gauge the amount of inventory that is being held by the company on its balance sheet at any point in time. So, for example, if the cost of sales for a company is €12,000, and if the value of inventory held is €1,000, then the company is holding sufficient inventory to trade for approximately one month. Inventory turnover can usefully be expressed in terms of the number of days of inventory that are held, which is calculated as follows.

$$\text{Inventory turnover} = \frac{\text{Inventory}}{\text{Cost of sales}} \times 365 \text{ days}$$

Similar logic can be applied to another key asset, accounts receivable. If a company's accounts receivable can be reduced, then the need for capital is lower, and so the ROIC is higher. Accounts receivable arise when a company has made a sale but not yet collected cash from its customers. The shorter the time from the recognition of a sale to the collection of cash, the lower is the accounts receivable balance. Accounts receivable turnover can therefore usefully be expressed in terms of the number of days taken to receive payment. Specifically, if we take the value of accounts receivable from the balance sheet, expressed as a proportion of the total sales recognised in the statement, then we can apply this proportion to the number of days in the year to determine the time taken to receive payment.

$$\text{Accounts receivable turnover} = \frac{\text{Accounts receivable}}{\text{Sales}} \times 365 \text{ days}$$

The common feature of sales per square metre, inventory turnover and accounts receivable turnover is the link between an item on the balance sheet and its counterpart in the income statement, in each case to provide insight into asset turnover. Taken together with a range of metrics relating to profit margin in the income statement, these metrics all provide insights that help to understand and to manage the ROIC that a company is able to achieve.

Economic profit

The discussion so far in this chapter has: first, identified that growth and value creation are not synonymous; second, introduced the concept of return on invested capital; and, third, shown that the evaluation of the determinants of the ROIC require data from both the income statement and the balance sheet. A fourth consideration, with which we will conclude the chapter, is how to assess whether any given level of ROIC represents a strong or weak performance.

The investor's concern is not just with making a positive ROIC, but also with the return being a good one in relation to other investment opportunities. The investments above in Table 6.1 generated a 10 per cent return, which increases the net worth of investors by €100k, but this is only a good outcome if the investor could not have put the money elsewhere and earned a higher return. For the same reason, you would rather keep your bank balance in a savings account rather than a checking account, and you regard the return offered by the latter as insufficient.

The value foregone by choosing one course of action over another is called the opportunity cost. If, in the example in Table 6.1 above, the €1,000k initial investment could have been made elsewhere, say in Company D as opposed to Company A, and if the ROIC in Company D had been 12 per cent, then the opportunity cost would be €120k. By the end of the first year the investor would have been better off by €20k had they invested in Company D. If your bank balance is €5,000, which you keep in a checking account at a 1 per cent rate of interest, as opposed to a savings account returning 4 per cent, then you will earn €50 in interest, but your opportunity cost is €200. You will be €50 better off by the end of the year, but you could have been €200 better off had you taken the better opportunity.

The shareholders' opportunity cost – the return that they could achieve by investing elsewhere – is typically referred to as the cost of capital. The underlying idea is that when the managers of a company raise capital from shareholders, there is an implicit understanding that the shareholders' money is being tied up and made unavailable for use elsewhere, which leads to an opportunity cost. Managers understand that capital is costly in this way, and it is on this basis that shareholders are willing to invest.

If the actual return that is achieved by an investment exceeds the opportunity cost of that investment, then we say that value is created. This is what CEOs mean when they talk about shareholder value creation. If, for example, an acquisition is justified on the basis that it creates shareholder value, the underlying reasoning is that, through synergy benefits or similar, the acquiring company is able to generate returns above the cost of capital that would not be achievable if the acquisition did not take place.

Economic profit is an accounting measure that captures the notion of value creation. A company is able to earn a profit because it has raised capital from shareholders to invest in assets. It follows that the shareholders' investment in the company was the right decision only if the profit earned by the company exceeds the opportunity cost or, as defined below, if economic profit is positive.

Economic profit = Profit − Cost of capital employed
= Profit − (Capital employed × % cost of capital)

It is important to note that economic profit is a notional amount. It is not associated with a transaction or event, and so it is not captured in a journal entry and is not reported in the financial statements. The important point is that value creation depends not just upon the amount of profit that a company makes but also on the amount of capital that is invested in order to make that profit. In this respect, while economic profit is not a number that is reported in the financial statements, it is a better measure than profit alone.

It is also worth noting that a company can grow even if it fails to make an economic profit. This can be achieved in one of two ways. First, so long as a company makes a profit, which is retained and reinvested, then the company will grow, whether or not the amount of profit achieved exceeds the cost of capital. Second, a company can in principle always grow by means of external funding, whether or not it is currently profitable.

We can conclude this discussion by looking at the worked examples in Tables 6.2 and 6.3, which extend the earlier example from Table 6.1. You should first refer back to Table 6.1. Assuming a cost of capital of 10 per cent, have a go at calculating the economic profit for each company in each year. You can then compare your answers with those in Table 6.2. Before reading on, try explaining the intuition behind the numbers that you have calculated: what is the meaning of the economic profit in each case?

Table 6.2 Economic profit

		Company A			Company B			Company C		
		Year 1 €k	Year 2 €k	Year 3 €k	Year 1 €k	Year 2 €k	Year 3 €k	Year 1 €k	Year 2 €k	Year 3 €k
Profit		100	100	100	100	110	121	0	0	0
Assets		1,000	1,000	1,000	1,000	1,100	1,210	1,000	1,100	1,210
Cost of capital	10%	100	100	100	100	110	121	100	110	121
Economic profit		**0**	**0**	**0**	**0**	**0**	**0**	**-100**	**-110**	**-121**

Table 6.3 Variation in economic profit

		Company A			Company B			Company C		
		Year 1 €k	Year 2 €k	Year 3 €k	Year 1 €k	Year 2 €k	Year 3 €k	Year 1 €k	Year 2 €k	Year 3 €k
Profit		100	100	100	100	110	121	0	0	0
Assets		1,000	1,000	1,000	1,000	1,100	1,210	1,000	1,100	1,210
Cost of capital	8%	80	80	80	80	88	96.8	80	88	96.8
Economic profit		**20**	**20**	**20**	**20**	**22**	**24**	**-80**	**-88**	**-97**

Table 6.2 can be interpreted as follows. Company A makes a 10 per cent return on capital, which is equal to the cost of capital, with the effect that economic profit is zero. The economic position of the shareholders would have been no different if they had invested their money elsewhere. Similarly, Company B also achieves an economic profit of zero each year, yet it differs from Company A because its profits grow. As we have seen earlier, however, the growth comes from retained profits, which is in substance a new investment made by shareholders. This higher level of shareholder investment leads to a higher cost of capital, which exactly offsets the higher profit. Company C, in contrast, generates an economic loss, which increases over time. The loss arises because the company incurred a cost of capital but it does not make any profit, and the loss increases because there is an increased investment of shareholders' capital yet the company remains unprofitable.

To conclude this analysis of economic profit, take a look now at Table 6.3, which differs from Table 6.2 in that the cost of capital is now lower, at 8 per cent.

Companies A and B now make a return on capital in excess of the cost of capital, with the effect that both generate an economic profit. Unlike in Table 6.2, however, the economic performance of the two companies differs, and Company B is now the better investment because its economic profit rises over time. The reason for this is that Company B is reinvesting shareholders funds at a return of 10 per cent, while Company A is returning cash to shareholders, who are only able to achieve a return of 8 per cent by reinvesting this money elsewhere. The general principle is that shareholders are better off the more that they invest in a company, whether by the retention of profit or the injection of new share capital, so long as the profit that the company is able to generate exceeds the cost of capital. This principle also applies, of course, in the opposite case, as illustrated by Company C: companies should in principle repay money to their shareholders if they are unable to invest at a profit that exceeds the cost of capital.

In summary

This chapter has shown that the creation of economic value is not measured by the growth of a business, nor even by the amount of the profit that the business generates. What matters is the amount of profit that is earned in relation to the capital that is employed. Specifically, value is created if the business can achieve a greater return on capital employed than would otherwise be achievable in an alternative investment.

All of this requires, of course, that we can measure profit, capital employed and the cost of capital. There is, however, subjectivity in practice in the measurement of each of these variables, and we have seen examples of this in earlier chapters. It is important, therefore, to take care in interpreting either the return on invested capital or economic profit, and in particular to seek to understand any subjectivity in the determination of profit and any ways in which the balance sheet fails to capture the economic value of net assets/capital employed.

7 Understanding risk

Understanding Risk

The last two chapters have reviewed growth and profitability. A further attribute of economic performance is risk: a given level of return on capital is more desirable if it can be achieved with a lower level of risk.

Any organisation faces a variety of risks, the financial effects of which are manifested in the financial statements. If, for example, customer demand is lower than expected, or if budgets for operating expenses are exceeded, or if changes in market prices cause the value of assets to decline, then profitability will be adversely affected.

The financial statements do more, however, than simply record the financial consequences of risks. They also, to some extent, provide information about exposure to risk, and in particular whether the financial structure of the business is itself inherently risky. We have already seen, for example, that if the assets on a balance sheet are relatively liquid, then the organisation is exposed to fewer risks, because the assets can more readily be diverted to alternative use if such need arises unexpectedly.

This chapter will illustrate two specific examples of using the financial statements to better understand exposure to risk. Specifically, we will explore operating leverage and financial leverage.

Operating leverage

Operating leverage is concerned with the risks inherent in an organisation's cost structure. To illustrate, consider Table 7.1, which presents a simplified statement of operating activities for two companies, A and B; specifically, there is an extract of an income statement, from revenue down to operating profit. The expenses incurred in running the business are divided into two categories: variable costs and fixed costs. This is an important distinction, which was mentioned briefly in Chapter 1 and which we will now explore more fully.

Table 7.1 Operating leverage

	Company	
	A €k	B €k
Revenue	5,000	5,000
Variable costs	250	4,000
Gross profit	4,750	1,000
Gross margin %	95%	20%
Fixed costs	4,000	250
Operating profit	750	750
Operating profit margin	15%	15%

Variable costs, by definition, are those that vary with output. Whenever a retail company makes a sale, for example, it also incurs a cost, equal to the value of the inventory that has been transferred into the possession of the customer. Likewise, the materials that make up a product are ultimately transferred from a manufacturing company to a customer at the point of sale, and it is at this point that both revenue and cost of goods sold are recognised in the income statement. Viewed in this way, variable costs are incurred only when a company generates output, and so revenue.

In contrast, fixed costs do not vary with output but are instead incurred over a period of time, whether or not there is output during that period. So, for example, if a retail company occupies a building and pays an annual rent, its income statement will include rental expenses whether or not the company actually makes any sales. Similarly, if a precondition of being open for business is that the retail company has to light and heat the building, employ sales staff and pay a fixed local business tax, and if all of these costs are incurred whether or not sales are made, then these costs are fixed rather than variable.

The difference between Company A and Company B in Table 7.1 is in the split between fixed and variable costs. Before reading on, you should consider whether this difference matters. After all, both companies generate the same revenue and make the same operating profit, so why might one cost structure be preferable to the other?

Companies A and B can be described as having different business models. Company A has a very high gross margin. For every €100 of sales, it incurs only €5 of variable costs and makes a gross profit of

€95. Moreover, as fixed costs do not vary with output, each €100 of sales not only adds €95 to gross profit but also to operating profit. Each sale can therefore be viewed as highly profitable. The difficulty for Company A, however, is that it has high fixed costs, amounting to 80 per cent of the current level of revenue, although its operating profit is positive overall because gross profit exceeds fixed costs. For Company B, the cost structure is reversed. The company achieves a relatively small gross margin of 20 per cent, yet it also has very significantly fewer fixed costs to cover and, at the current level of revenue, while its gross profit is less than that of company A, its operating profit is the same.

The relationship between variable costs and fixed costs is measured by a ratio called operating leverage (or operating gearing). Operating leverage can be defined as follows.

$$\text{Operating leverage (gearing)} = \frac{\text{Fixed costs}}{\text{Total costs (fixed + variable)}}$$

High operating leverage might be found in industries where a large amount of investment in plant and equipment is required. Consider, for example, a telecom network, where a huge investment in infrastructure and running costs has to be made before any revenue can be earned, yet where the variable costs incurred when a customer uses the network are very small in relation to the price that is charged. Similarly, a hotel must incur high fixed costs in order simply to be open for business, yet the price it can charge for a room is significantly higher than any variable costs it incurs as a result of guests using the room. Other industries provide further examples, for example airlines or car rental companies.

Low operating leverage can be found, for example, in supermarkets, where the business model involves high turnover at low margins, leading to high variable costs. Other forms of business that provide a bridge between wholesale and retail markets behave similarly, for example brokers or distributors, which typically trade at low margins but high volumes.

The importance of operating leverage becomes apparent when we consider the impact on a company's profits from varying its level of output, as illustrated in Table 7.2. At current levels of output, there is no difference in operating profit between Company A and Company B, yet because each company differs significantly in its operating leverage, any change in output has a significantly different effect.

Table 7.2 Effects of operating leverage

	Company		Volume doubles		Volume halves	
	A €k	B €k	A €k	B €k	A €k	B €k
Revenue	5,000	5,000	10,000	10,000	2,500	2,500
Variable costs	250	4,000	500	8,000	125	2,000
Gross profit	4,750	1,000	9,500	2,000	2,375	500
Gross margin %	95%	20%	95%	20%	95%	20%
Fixed costs	4,000	250	4,000	250	4,000	250
Operating profit	750	750	5,500	1,750	-1,625	250
Operating profit margin	15%	15%	55%	18%	-65%	10%

Company A has high operating leverage (94 per cent). If it fails to generate any sales, it will make a large loss that is equal to its fixed costs. On the other hand, each sale that it makes is highly profitable. Once it has generated sufficient sales to achieve a gross profit equal to its fixed costs, and so to break even, then additional sales lead to a rapid accumulation of operating profit. Company A can therefore be seriously loss-making when volume is low, but especially profitable when volume is high. In other words, it is risky, because profit varies considerably with market conditions.

Company B, in contrast, does not lose much money if it fails to achieve breakeven volume, because the fixed costs are very low. On the other hand, any output that it achieves above the breakeven level contributes only to a gradual accumulation of operating profit, because the variable cost of each sale is so high. It is less risky than Company A: profits are not so high when times are good, but neither are they so low (or negative) when times are bad. In the extreme case, a company which has zero fixed costs also has zero risk of making an operating loss, because even at zero output it has no costs, and because presumably it will only make a sale if the revenue exceeds the variable cost.

This discussion is illustrated in Figure 7.1, which shows breakeven charts for companies A and B. Notice that while the relationship between revenue and output is the same for Company A as for Company B, the relationship between cost and output is different. In comparison with Company B, Company A's total costs are high in relation to revenue when output is low, but they become relatively low

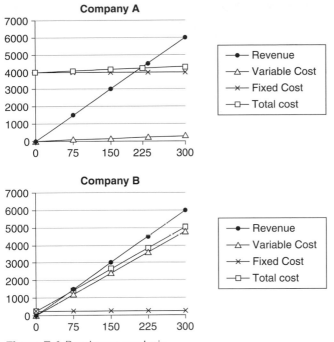

Figure 7.1 Breakeven analysis

as revenue increases. Profit is measured by the vertical difference between the revenue line and the total cost. At low levels of output, Company A's losses exceed those of Company B. Company A is also slower to reach breakeven. Yet at higher levels of output, Company A becomes significantly more profitable.

The amount added to profit by each incremental unit of output is called a contribution. It is equal to the sales price per unit less the variable cost per unit. The idea is that this amount contributes to covering fixed costs. Each incremental sale makes a contribution, and breakeven is reached once the sum of these contributions is equal to the fixed cost.

As an exercise in confirming your understanding of Figure 7.1, you might like to calculate the breakeven point for each of the two companies. This is the level of output at which the fixed cost equals the total contribution. You will know if you have the right answer because, at the breakeven output level, revenue (i.e. unit price multiplied by output) is equal to total cost (i.e. fixed cost, plus variable cost per unit multiplied by output).

We have seen that high operating leverage causes the amount of profit earned to be relatively sensitive to the volume of sales generated. One implication of this is that companies with high operating leverage are particularly sensitive to the economic cycle. While all companies experience fluctuations in sales as general economy activity cycles up and down, this variation in sales causes an amplified variation in profit for companies with high operating leverage. Investors therefore classify such companies as cyclical: they recover strongly when the economy is coming out of recession, and they perform particularly well during a boom, but they are also particularly badly hit during a downturn.

Operating leverage has implications for economic decision making. So long as each incremental sale generates a positive contribution, it will lead to an increase in profit. This has direct consequences for pricing behaviour. Consider, for example, a hotel, which has high operating leverage. Each time that the hotel sells a room for the night, it incurs a modest variable cost, to cover activities such as cleaning and servicing the room. The price that it can charge for the room is likely to be significantly higher than this variable cost. Indeed, the price must, on average, be significantly higher in order to make a sufficient contribution to cover the high fixed costs. Suppose, however, that a hotel has a standard room rate of €200 and a variable cost per room of €20 – i.e. a contribution of €180 per room, or a 90 per cent gross margin – but that, on a given night, it cannot sell all of its rooms at the standard rate, with 20 rooms remaining vacant. If it reduced the rate to €150, however, it would sell 15 of these, and at a further reduction to €50, it would sell the remaining 5 rooms. What, in your view, should the hotel do?

The first thing to note is that, even at a price of €50, the hotel is able to make a positive contribution, of €30 per room. All else remaining equal, the hotel's profit for the night would be €150 higher if it sold its final 5 rooms at €50 each, as opposed to leaving them vacant. On the same basis, selling the other 15 rooms would increase profit by a further €130 per room, or €1,950 in total. If, then, the hotel retains its standard rate of €200, but reduces this where necessary to achieve full occupancy, overall profit increases by €2,100.

In this case, the hotel would be practising what is called price discrimination, which is a targeted method of pricing, whereby the same product is sold at different prices to different customers, according to their willingness to pay. This requires, of course, that the hotel's ability to charge €200 per night is not undermined by its practice of sometimes charging less. Additionally, and for the policy to make economic sense, the hotel must have high gross profit margins, giving it the flexibility to reduce prices while still making a positive contribution. In other words, price discrimination goes hand in hand with high operating leverage. You are likely to have had experiences in booking hotel rooms, rental cars or airline seats, where the price seems either unusually high or surprisingly low, with considerable variation that can be difficult to understand. You may also have been overwhelmed by the variety of pricing plans, discount schemes and the like in these sectors, and also in other sectors such as telecom, electricity or gas, where you always seem to be offered a better deal yet nevertheless feel that you may be overpaying. The underlying reason for this pricing behaviour is high operating leverage: the aim of the supplier is to charge the highest price possible, in order to maximise total contribution in order to cover fixed costs and make a profit. Yet on any individual sale, a positive contribution typically remains possible even with a very significant reduction in price. Contrast this with an organisation that has very low operating leverage, where the gross margin is tight. In such a case, it does not make economic sense to reduce the price by very much, because to do so would lead to a negative contribution. The scope of price discrimination is thereby significantly reduced, although so too is the need, because the nature of the business model is that there are fewer fixed costs to cover.

Operating leverage: some caveats

The analysis above of operating leverage suggests some important insights regarding the financial consequences of the fixed-variable split in an organisation's cost structure. In practice, however, it is very difficult to make this split in a clean and unambiguous way. This is for several reasons.

First, and most important, cost behaviour is not, in practice, as simple as we would like it to be. We have so far assumed that costs fall neatly into one of two categories: they either vary with output, in which case they are variable, or they are independent of output, in which case they are fixed. In practice, however, few costs are truly variable, and few are truly fixed. To illustrate this, it is helpful to introduce a further distinction, between direct costs and indirect costs.

	Indirect (overhead)	Direct
Variable	Variable overhead	Variable direct
Fixed	Fixed overhead	n/a

Figure 7.2 Cost categories

A direct cost can be defined as one that varies in direct proportion with output: a given percentage increase in output results in the same percentage increase in direct cost. One way to picture direct costs is to consider the manufacture and sale of cars. For every car sold, the manufacturer incurs the cost of the materials that go into the car. Hence, the engine, steering wheel, seats and so on, are all direct costs of car production because they are unambiguously attributable to units of output. In contrast, an indirect cost, otherwise known as an overhead, does not vary in direct proportion with output. For example, the costs of the car company's senior management team, marketing activities, R&D function, and so on, change relatively little in response to changes in the number of cars sold.

The distinction between direct and indirect costs is similar to that between variable and fixed costs, yet there is an important difference. Consider Figure 7.2, which shows the relationship between these two different classifications of cost. All direct costs are necessarily variable, because an extra direct cost is only incurred when there is an extra unit of output. All fixed costs, meanwhile, are necessarily indirect, because they have no relationship with output. These two categories – direct/variable and indirect/fixed – were the only categories that we considered above in the breakeven analysis. Yet there is a third category – variable/indirect, or variable overhead – which comprises costs that increase as volume increases (i.e. they are variable, not fixed) yet they do not increase in direct proportion with output (i.e. they are indirect, not direct). Many costs fall into this category in practice: as organisations expand the scale of their activities and outputs, so their cost base expands also, yet rarely can the growth in various overhead activities, such as IT, marketing, HR, facilities and so on, be linked directly to output. Moreover, the fixed-variable boundary can change over time. While a fixed cost is one that does not vary over a particular period of time, the longer the time period that is under consideration, the less likely it is that the cost will be fixed. Over a long enough period of time all costs can be considered to be variable. Even within a relatively short time period it is possible for the cost structure to change. If, for example, a company ceases to manufacture a component part itself, and outsources to a supplier, then it may unburden itself of the overheads of that activity, instead only paying per component for whatever it consumes. In other words, it converts overheads to direct costs.

In practice, while it is a reasonable working assumption to regard an organisation's cost of goods sold as variable, and all other expenses in the income statement as fixed, this is at best only an approximation. Companies are not actually formally required to make a distinction, for external reporting purposes, between fixed and variable costs, because the distinction is too ambiguous to be readily and meaningfully enforced. And even within a company's own, internal financial reporting systems, any fixed-variable distinction should be treated with caution.

In general, operating leverage is a valuable analytical tool, along with the associated distinctions between costs that are fixed or variable, and direct or indirect. Unavoidably, however, simple classifications of costs are imprecise and ambiguous, and they should be applied accordingly.

Financial leverage

We have seen that profit can vary according to the level of a company's operating leverage. A similar conclusion holds also for financial leverage, which concerns the relationship between equity and debt in the financing of a company. Financial leverage is typically defined as the value of debt on the balance sheet divided by the total value of capital employed (i.e. debt plus equity), as follows.

$$\text{Financial leverage (gearing)} = \frac{\text{Debt}}{\text{Capital Employed}} = \frac{\text{Debt}}{\text{Debt} + \text{Equity}}$$

The similarity between operating and financial leverage lies in the implications for shareholders' economic returns of the existence of fixed costs. With operating leverage, we have seen that relatively high fixed costs increase the sensitivity of profit to changes in output. With financial leverage, a relatively high amount of debt leads to a relatively high interest expense, which is a fixed cost during a period of time. As with operating leverage, the effect of this high fixed cost is to

Table 7.3 Financial leverage

	A €k	B €k	C €k
Income	55	55	55
Expenses	–5	–5	–5
Operating profit	50	50	50
Interest expense	–5	–10	–20
Profit	45	40	30
Assets	500	500	500
Loan	100	200	400
Equity	400	300	100
Capital employed	500	500	500
Return on capital employed (ROCE)	10.0%	10.0%	10.0%
Return on equity (ROE)	11.3%	13.3%	30.0%
Return on debt (rate of interest)	5.0%	5.0%	5.0%

amplify variations in profitability resulting from variations in business performance.

Table 7.3 provides an illustrative example of the effects of financial leverage. Each company – A, B and C – operates in the real estate business. These companies raise capital from shareholders and the bank, purchase buildings and make a profit by renting those buildings for an amount that exceeds operating expenses and interest expenses. You should first take a look at Company A, which has total capital employed of €500k, made up of €400k shareholders' capital and a €100k bank loan. The company therefore has total assets of €500k, which are comprised entirely of buildings. The company generates rental income of €55k, against which it incurs various expenses amounting to €5k, such that the net return from renting the buildings is €50k. The rate of interest on the bank loan is 5 per cent, meaning that the interest expense is €5k, and the company's profit is €45k. For simplicity, it is assumed that the company pays no taxes.

The profit of €45k that is earned after the payment of interest belongs entirely to the equity investor. The capital invested by shareholders was €400k, and the return on this capital is therefore 11.3 per cent. This is called the return on equity, or ROE, which is defined as the bottom line of the income statement (i.e. profit after tax) divided by equity. (In our simplified example, there is no tax, and so profit before tax and profit after tax are one and the same.)

$$\text{Return on equity (ROE)} = \frac{\text{Profit after tax}}{\text{Equity}}$$

Take a look now at Companies B and C in Table 7.3. You will see that the only difference among the balance sheets of these companies is in the percentage split between debt and equity in total capital employed. In other words, the difference is in what is termed capital structure.

At one extreme, a company's capital could be entirely comprised of equity, making it 100 per cent equity-financed. If, however, a company takes on debt finance in addition to equity, then it is said to be leveraged, or geared. The idea is that shareholders are leveraging up, or gearing up, their own investment by borrowing from others, so creating a larger business than would otherwise have been possible. The shareholders in Company A, for example, have invested €400k of their own money, and by borrowing a further €100k from the bank, they have created a business with assets of €500k. Company B's shareholders have only invested €300k of their own money, yet they have leveraged this to a greater degree and they, too, have created a business with assets of €500k. Using the definition provided above, the financial leverage for Companies A, B and C is, respectively, 20 per cent, 40 per cent and 80 per cent.

There are two consequences of this difference in financial leverage. The first is that Companies B and C have higher interest expenses than Company A, leading to a lower profit. The second is that the profit generated by Companies B and C is attributable to a smaller amount of equity capital than is the case for Company A. The first of these two differences causes the ROE to be lower, since the numerator (profit) is smaller, while the second difference causes the ROE to be higher, since the denominator (equity) is also smaller. In our example, the second of these two effects is greater than the first, making the ROE for Company B, at 13.3 per cent, higher than that of Company A, while the ROE for Company C is higher still, at 30 per cent.

In general, Table 7.3 reports a positive relationship between financial leverage and ROE: the more that shareholders borrow, the higher is the return on their investment. Before reading on, you should pause to consider why this might be the case. Try making an analogy with your own decision when buying a house: do you achieve a greater return on your investment the more that you borrow? If so, why is that the case, and if not, why not?

The answer lies in two other measures of return on invested capital, other than the ROE, both of which are reported in Table 7.3. These are the return on capital employed (ROCE) and the return on debt (i.e. the interest expense). As we will see, it is actually the relationship between these three measures of return that determines the effect of financial leverage.

ROCE is a measure of the total return generated by the combined investment of debt and equity capital, regardless of the balance between the two. The denominator in this calculation is capital employed, which is 500 for all three of our companies. The numerator is operating profit, because this is the net amount that is generated by the company's assets and that is available to distribute to providers of finance. In the case of Company A, for example, the net gain from renting its buildings is €50k, of which €5k is a return to the providers of debt capital and €45k is a return to the providers of equity capital. So, we have the following calculation.

$$\text{Return on capital employed (ROCE)} = \frac{\text{Operating profit}}{\text{Capital employed (debt + equity)}}$$

You will have noticed that both operating profit and the return on capital employed are the same for each of our three companies. This is because the difference between the companies is not in the value of the assets that they hold, nor in the returns generated by those assets, but instead only in their capital structures, which do not form part of the ROCE calculation. Alternatively stated, the business of buying and renting out buildings generates a return of 10 per cent. This is the operating performance. It is a measure of the intrinsic profitability of the business. Our three companies differ in their return on equity not because of differences in the quality of the investments that they have made, but instead because of differences in the way in which those investments have been financed.

Of the two components of capital employed, the return to shareholders is measured by the ROE, while the return to the bank is measured by the rate of interest. In Table 7.3, the bank has invested €100k and has received an income of €5k in return, making the rate of interest (i.e. the return on debt) equal to 5 per cent.

There are two key differences between the return on shareholders' capital and the return on the bank's capital. The first is that the financial statements are designed with shareholders in mind. Profit is a change in equity. It is a measure of how much wealthier shareholders have become during the reporting period. By definition, income increases shareholders' wealth and expenses reduce shareholders' wealth. While the return on shareholders' capital and the return on the bank's capital are both measures of the gains made by investing in the business, the former is profit while the latter is an expense that is deducted in the calculation of profit. The second difference is that the return on the bank's capital is a contractually agreed amount, whether at a fixed or variable rate of interest, while the return on shareholders' capital is simply the residual after deducting all expenses from income, meaning that it could in principle be any amount, positive or negative.

We can now return to the question of why the ROE in Table 7.3 increases as leverage increases. The critical relationship here is between the ROCE and the rate of interest. If the former is greater than the latter, which is the case for all three of our companies, then the operating profit generated by investing in the business is greater than the cost of borrowing to make that investment. It follows that any amount of borrowing is profitable, and that the more that is borrowed, the better. The rate of return made by the bank is fixed, while that made by shareholders is not. If the shareholders invest only a small amount of their own money, while making profits on a large amount of borrowed money, then the percentage return on their investment will be high. This is what is happening in Table 7.3. The return on equity for Company C is significantly higher than that for Company A because the effect of leverage is that a greater amount of profit is being made in relation to the amount invested.

Consider your own decision when buying a house. If you buy a €500,000 house entirely with your own money, and if the value of the house increases to €600,000, then you have made a 20 per cent return on your investment. If, alternatively, you invest €100,000 of your own money and borrow €400,000 from the bank at a rate of interest of 10 per cent, then your gain will be €60,000 (i.e. the gain on the house less €40,000 interest expense), which is a 60 per cent return on your investment.

The ROE therefore has two components. First, it depends upon the inherent profitability of the business, as measured by the ROCE. In the house example just given, this is 20 per cent. Second, it depends upon the way in which business is financed, as measured by financial leverage. In the house example, the effect of leverage is to increase the return to 60 per cent. In making a comparison between different companies, it is helpful to keep these two components separate from one another. The inherent profitability of the industry or sector, and the effectiveness of the management team in generating operating profit in relation to other companies in the sector, are better measured by the ROCE rather than by the ROE. This is because the former is concerned exclusively with the business, while the latter mixes up business performance with the effects of financial leverage.

Before completing our discussion of financial leverage, you should pause to consider whether the effect of leverage is always positive. Specifically, what would it take for the picture in Table 7.3 to be reversed, such that the relationship between leverage and ROE becomes negative?

Again, the critical relationship here is between the ROCE and the rate of interest. If, instead of being positive, the difference between these two measures becomes negative, such that the return generated by the business is lower than the cost of borrowing, then the more that a business borrows, the lower will be its ROE. This is illustrated in Table 7.4. For Companies D, E and F, operating performance is the same as for Companies A, B and C, but the rate of interest, at 15 per cent, is now higher than the ROCE. The effect is that while there are still profits being made at low levels of financial leverage, the position becomes loss-making as leverage increases. Moreover, a loss of €10k is incurred by shareholders of Company F on an investment of only €100k, and so the effect of leverage is to turn a positive 10 per cent ROCE into a negative 10 per cent ROE.

The relationship that we have uncovered here is between risk and return. The more that shareholders leverage up their investment, the greater is the potential variation in ROE. If the business performs well (i.e. ROCE is high), a greater amount of leverage leads to a higher ROE. If the business performs badly, shareholders will lose a greater percentage of their investment if they have borrowed more heavily. If, as illustrated in the cases of Companies G, H and I, the return on the business is equal to the cost of debt (i.e. ROCE = rate of interest), then the extent of financial leverage no longer matters, because the benefits to shareholders from the returns generated by investing the bank's money are exactly equal to the cost of borrowing that money.

We can complete this discussion by returning to consider your decision to borrow in order to buy a house. Suppose that you have already decided to buy a house that costs €500,000, and that your only remaining decision is whether to finance the purchase entirely with your own money (equity) or whether to take out a mortgage (debt)

Table 7.4 Effects of financial leverage

	ROCE less than rate of interest			ROCE = rate of interest		
	D **€k**	**E** **€k**	**F** **€k**	**G** **€k**	**H** **€k**	**I** **€k**
Income	55	55	55	55	55	55
Expenses	−5	−5	−5	−5	−5	−5
Operating profit	50	50	50	50	50	50
Interest expense	−15	−30	−60	−10	−20	−40
Profit	35	20	−10	40	30	10
Assets	500	500	500	500	500	500
Loan	100	200	400	100	200	400
Equity	400	300	100	400	300	100
	500	500	500	500	500	500
Return on capital employed (ROCE)	10.0%	10.0%	10.0%	10.0%	10.0%	10.0%
Return on equity (ROE)	8.8%	6.7%	−10.0%	10.0%	10.0%	10.0%
Return on debt (rate of interest)	15.0%	15.0%	15.0%	10.0%	10.0%	10.0%

and, if so, how large the mortgage should be. Suppose that the rate of interest on the mortgage is fixed at 10 per cent and suppose also, to keep the example simple, that the operating profit from the house is measured simply by the change in its market value, such that your profit as the homeowner (i.e. the increase in equity on your personal balance sheet) is equal to the increase in market value less the interest payment on your mortgage. As Table 7.5 illustrates, the decision that you need to make is in principle very simple. If you believe that the rate of increase in house prices (i.e. the ROCE) will exceed the rate of interest, then you should borrow. And the greater your willingness to take on risk, the more you should borrow. Before reading further, take a look at each of the examples in Table 7.5 to see these effects at work.

In scenario A, there is only a small increase in house prices, such that the ROCE is less than the rate of interest. As there is only 20 per cent leverage, however, the interest expense is small and it is exceeded by the modest operating profit. Overall, therefore, there is a small ROE of 1.3 per cent. In contrast, scenario B combines high

Table 7.5 Financial leverage when buying a house

	A €k	B €k	C €k	D €k	E €k	F €k
Asset (cost of house)	500	500	500	500	500	500
House price increase % (ROCE)	2.5%	2.5%	7.5%	7.5%	12.5%	12.5%
Operating profit	12.5	12.5	37.5	37.5	62.5	62.5
Liability (mortgage)	100	300	100	300	100	300
Rate of interest	7.5%	7.5%	7.5%	7.5%	7.5%	7.5%
Interest expense	−7.5	−22.5	−7.5	−22.5	−7.5	−22.5
Equity	400	200	400	200	400	200
Profit	5	−10	30	15	55	40
Return on equity (ROE)	1.3%	−5.0%	7.5%	7.5%	13.8%	20.0%

leverage with low ROCE. In this case, the risk taken by borrowing heavily has proved unfavourable and there is a loss of €10k and a negative 5 per cent ROE. In scenarios C and D, the ROCE is equal to the rate of interest, with the effect that both are equal to the ROE, regardless of the level of leverage. Profit is higher under scenario C because interest expenses are lower, yet the level of equity investment is correspondingly lower also, such that ROE is unaffected. Finally, scenarios E and F comprise an ROCE in excess of the rate of interest, with the effect that higher leverage leads to higher ROE. In scenario E, where leverage its low, the ROE of 13.8 per cent is only marginally higher than the ROCE of 12.5 per cent, while the high leverage in scenario F leads to an ROE as high as 20 per cent.

In summary

This chapter has demonstrated how the financial statements can provide information on the inherent financial risks of an organisation. Specifically, the rate of return earned by shareholders (ROE) is sensitive to two forms of leverage, operating and financial. When conditions are favourable, a high ratio of fixed costs to total costs (operating leverage) and a high ratio of debt to equity (financial leverage) both contribute to abnormally high returns on equity, while the effect is reversed when conditions are unfavourable; leverage and volatility of financial performance go hand in hand.

The financial statements do not, of course, present a complete picture of the risks of business enterprise. It is not possible to infer, from the financial statements alone, the nature of the various risks that a business faces with respect to its customers, employees, suppliers, product development, competitors and so on. It is, however, possible to use the financial statements to understand the inherent risks of operating leverage and financial leverage, as well as to better understand the financial consequences of the broader risks to which the organisation is exposed. As ever, the financial statements are an important part of the overall story, and the basis from which to increase understanding and to identify areas to explore further, but they can only be a part of the picture, and not the whole.

Building a corporate valuation model

Building a Corporate Valuation Model

We know from previous chapters that the financial statements record such things as how a business has been financed, what investments it has made in assets and, over time, how much profit it has earned from those assets. The financial statements can therefore be described as historical: they report what has happened, and not what is expected to happen. This historical role does not, however, imply that accounting information is not relevant to understanding, and making decisions about, what is expected to happen in the future. Indeed, the opposite is very much the case, and in this chapter we will explore a forward-looking role for accounting information. In particular, we will build a model in which forecasts of financial statement data are used to determine the valuation of a company.

We can start by identifying three reasons why accounting information can usefully play a forward-looking role in financial analysis and decision-making.

The first reason is that, to the extent that the future can be predicted based upon realised outcomes in the past, accounting data can provide the foundation for making financial forecasts. Indeed, it is not obvious how else the future can be predicted other than by some form of extrapolation from the past. So, for example, a good starting point in forecasting sales revenue is to consider the sales that have actually been achieved in recent years.

The second reason, which is perhaps less obvious but no less important, is that the accounting model provides a coherent framework within which to structure assumptions and data about future financial performance. So, for example, if a company forecasts growth in sales, then it must implicitly be assuming growth in other variables as well, such as the value of additional assets employed to generate those incremental sales, and in turn the financing required to acquire those assets. As this chapter will illustrate, the financial statements provide a logical structure with which to ensure that these various assumptions about different aspects of a business are made consistently with one another.

The third reason is that financial forecasts form part of a feedback loop that also involves financial control and the measurement of realised financial performance. Specifically, budgets are a specific type of financial forecast, being detailed plans in the form of short-term targets for financial performance. As actual financial performance is realised over time, budgets are used as a mechanism for monitoring and control. Departures from budget arise when actual performance differs from expected performance, and these departures provide information that can feed back into improving the forecasting process, leading to revised budgets for the next period ahead, and so the cycle continues. So, for example, if sales performance is ahead of budget, then this triggers an analysis of the reasons why, which, in turn, is likely to lead to future sales forecasts being revised, including the budget for the next period.

Having reviewed in previous chapters the use of accounting information to understand historical performance, we will now explore ways in which forecasts of the financial statements can be generated. We will start with the income statement and the balance sheet.

Forecasting the income statement and balance sheet

Forecasts for any individual item in the financial statements are likely to depend upon forecasts for other items, for example the forecasted volume of sales will determine the level of inventory that is expected to be required. Forecasting a set of financial statements is therefore an iterative process, with changes in certain assumptions and forecasts leading to changes in others until, finally, the forecasted financial statements become a coherent whole.

A reasonable starting point in this iterative process is to make forecasts for sales, and from there to develop forecasts for the income statement as a whole. In practice, forecasted sales are likely to be anchored heavily in the level of sales that have been achieved historically, although of course there are many factors that might cause sales in the future to differ from those in the past. These factors include changes in the competitive landscape, the launch of new products or services, additional sales resulting from newly acquired businesses, possible effects of new advertising campaigns or distribution channels or pricing strategies, and so on. Each of these factors illustrates the limitations of historical accounting information, and the need for forward-looking, non-financial information, yet the natural starting point from which to forecast sales is nevertheless the actual performance that the company has in practice been able to achieve.

The forecast for sales should be consistent with the forecasts made for other financial statement variables, and evidence from past financial statements can provide valuable checks in testing for this consistency. So, for example, if it is assumed that sales will grow by 10 per cent in each year, yet it is also assumed that operating expenses for advertising, new product development, sales representatives and customer relations all grow by only 4 per cent each year, then the implicit assumption is that the ratio of each of these expenses to sales will decline in relation to historical levels; this may therefore be an unrealistically optimistic set of assumptions. On the other hand, there may be a significant fixed cost element to each of these operating expenses, making it plausible that the total cost per unit of output declines as output increases – i.e. that there are economies of scale. In this case, a reduction in ratios of operating expenses to sales should be expected. To counter this argument again, however, it might well be the case that, in the past, the company has always expected to achieve economies of scale in the future, while experience suggests that it rarely actually does so in practice. In other words, the company has historically been too willing to believe that its costs were fixed, when in fact they would have been better described as variable overheads, which trended upwards in line with increasing sales. With each of these arguments and counter arguments, the accounting records cannot provide definitive answers, because they record historical performance and cannot anticipate the future; yet what the accounts can do is instil rigour into the forecasting process. They provide evidence of achieved levels of performance, including relationships between sales and expenses, as well as information on whether forecasts made in previous periods have proved to be systematically either optimistic or pessimistic.

Table 8.1 presents a very simple, five-year forecast for an income statement, where the only variables are sales, operating expenses, operating profit, tax and profit after tax. Among the simplifying assumptions in this example are that there is neither depreciation of property, plant and equipment (PPE) nor interest expenses arising from debt. The annual growth in sales is assumed to be in the range 5 per cent to 7 per cent per annum. The reason for this growth rate,

Table 8.1 Income statement

	Year 1 €k	Year 2 €k	Year 3 €k	Year 4 €k	Year 5 €k
Sales	750	788	833	885	945
Expenses	–525	–551	–583	–620	–662
Operating profit	225	236	250	266	284
Tax	–90	–95	–100	–106	–113
Profit after tax	135	142	150	159	170

which relates to the growth in PPE, will be discussed later. A simple assumption has been made for operating expenses, which is that they maintain a constant percentage relationship with sales. Specifically, expenses are assumed to be 70 per cent of sales in each year, making the operating profit margin 30 per cent. The tax rate is in turn assumed to be 40 per cent, making profit after tax 18 per cent of sales. These assumptions are illustrative only; it would, of course, be possible to make alternative assumptions for any of the variables in any of the years in the forecast.

Take a look now at the balance sheet in Table 8.2. As was the case for the income statement, this is a very simple illustration, yet it will suffice to demonstrate the fundamental characteristics of the financial forecast that is required for a business valuation. It is assumed that the PPE in the business grows at a modest rate each year. Specifically, €50k is added to the value of PPE in the first year, €60k in the second year, and so on. The only other asset of the business is accounts receivable, representing amounts already recognised in the income statement for which cash has yet to be received from customers. At the end of year one, the accounts receivable balance stands at €123k, which is an amount based upon an assumption that customer payment takes an average of 60 days – i.e. €123k is €750k × (60/365). This assumption is maintained throughout the five-year forecast, such that accounts receivable increase gradually in line with sales.

There is also an assumed relationship between PPE and sales. The assumption is that a given amount of PPE supports a given level of sales, such that any percentage increase in PPE at the end of the year causes the same percentage increase in sales in the following year. Hence, as mentioned above, it is the current level and forecasted growth of PPE in the balance sheet that is the basis for the current level and forecasted growth of sales in the income statement.

Table 8.2 Balance sheet

	Year 0 €	Year 1 €	Year 2 €	Year 3 €	Year 4 €	Year 5 €
PPE	1,000	1,050	1,110	1,180	1,260	1,260
Accounts receivable	118	123	129	137	145	155
Operating assets	**1,118**	**1,173**	**1,239**	**1,317**	**1,405**	**1,415**
Share capital	1,118	1,118	1,118	1,118	1,118	1,118
Retained profit	0	55	121	198	287	297
Equity	**1,118**	**1,173**	**1,239**	**1,317**	**1,405**	**1,415**

Specifically, it is assumed that each €1k invested in PPE in the closing balance sheet generates annual sales of €0.75k in the following year, making sales in the first year equal to €750k.

There is no debt in Table 8.2, nor any other form of liability, and so the value of net operating assets is necessarily equal to the value of equity. It is assumed that there is no issue or repurchase of share capital, such that all increases in equity are made up of increases in the balance of retained profit.

Try to work out why the balance of retained profit increases gradually from €0 in the opening balance sheet for the first year ('year 0') to €297k in the closing balance sheet for the fifth year ('year 5'). For example, why is the retained profit €55k at the end of the first year ('year 1'), and why does this increase to €121k by the end of the second year? In completing this exercise, you might find it helpful to work out what the company's cash flow statement looks like in each year. In doing this, you should note that the company's cash balance stands at zero at each balance sheet date, meaning that the bottom line of the cash flow statement (i.e. the change in cash) must also be zero in each period.

Once you have had a go at this exercise, continue to read the next section below, which presents the cash flow statement and discusses how it relates to the income statement and the balance sheet.

Forecasting the cash flow statement

As we already have forecasts for the income statement and the balance sheet, we can work out what the forecasts for the cash flow statement must look like. This is best seen by considering each category of the cash flow statement in turn, which we will do initially for the first year of the forecast.

In general, if all sales revenue is received in cash and if all expenses are paid in cash, then there will be no difference between operating cash flow and profit after tax. In this situation, each double entry that changes the profit/equity account will also change the cash account, and there will be no impact on any other asset or liability on the balance sheet.

We know from the balance sheet, however, that accounts receivable increased by €5k during the first year, implying that the cash received from sales must have been €5k less than the amount recognised in the income statement. In contrast, there is no such difference for expenses in our example, because there are no accounts payable. Overall, therefore, operating cash flow must be €130k, which is €5k less than profit after tax. The total change to the balance sheet in this context amounts to a credit to profit/equity of €135k, a debit to accounts receivable of €5k and a debit to cash of €130k.

Apart from the increase in accounts receivable, the other change in the balance sheet is the increase in PPE. This results from the acquisition of new PPE and it must therefore correspond to a negative investing cash flow. In year 1, the change in PPE, and therefore also the cash flow, is €50k: the double entry is a debit to PPE of €50k and a credit to cash of €50k, with no overall change in net assets.

If the operating cash inflow is €130k in year 1, while the investing cash outflow is €50k, then there is a surplus of €80k from the company's operating activities, and this surplus must either be paid back to providers of finance (which in this example must be the shareholders) or else it can be retained as a cash balance within the company. As we know that the cash balance was zero at the start and the end of the year, it follows that there must have been a cash payment of €80k to shareholders. In fact, we can see that this must have been the case, because the retained profit for the year is €55k, which equals the profit after tax of €135k less the dividend of €80k. The double entry here is a debit to retained profit of €80k and a credit to cash of €80k.

We have now completed the cash flow statement for the first year, and we can follow the same logic to determine the cash flow statement in each subsequent year. In the second year, for example, the operating cash inflow is €136k, which is equal to profit after tax of €142k less the increase in accounts receivable of €6k, while the investing cash outflow is €60k, which is the increase in PPE. Taking both of these cash flow categories together, there is a net cash inflow of €76k, which is equal to profit after tax of €142k less the total increase in operating

Table 8.3 Cash flow statement

	Year 1 €k	Year 2 €k	Year 3 €k	Year 4 €k	Year 5 €k
Operating	130	136	142	151	160
Investing	−50	−60	−70	−80	0
Financing	−80	−76	−72	−71	−160
Change in cash	0	0	0	0	0

assets (PPE and accounts receivable) of €66k. As this net cash inflow is not retained in the company's bank account but is instead paid out as a dividend, there is a financing cash outflow of €76k.

It is the financing cash outflow that the shareholders of the business are ultimately interested in, because it is only by receiving a dividend that they get cash back from the initial cash investment that they made to acquire shares in the company. While it is true, of course, that any given shareholder can also realise cash by selling their shares to another shareholder, the same is not true for all of the shareholders collectively: it is only when the company pays a dividend or repurchases shares that cash is transferred back out of the company to the shareholder body as a whole, marking the end of the investment cycle that started when shareholders initially parted with cash to purchase shares.

We have seen in our example that cash returned to shareholders is equal to the sum of operating cash flows and investing cash flows. We have also seen that, in each reporting period, this amount is equal to profit after tax less the increase in operating assets; you should check Tables 8.1, 8.2 and 8.3 to verify that this is the case. It follows that if we forecast the income statement, as we did in Table 8.1, and also the balance sheet, as we did in Table 8.2, then there is no need to also forecast the cash flow statement, because the overall cash flow that we are interested in can be determined by taking the bottom line of the income statement (profit after tax) and subtracting the change in operating assets from the opening to the closing balance sheets. This is illustrated in Table 8.4, where the cash metric discussed here is termed 'free cash flow'.

Our discussion of business valuation is now almost complete. There remains one important issue yet to be explored, which concerns the method by which the free cash flows generated by a company are valued by shareholders. As we shall see in the next section of this

Table 8.4 Determining free cash flow

	Year 1 €k	Year 2 €k	Year 3 €k	Year 4 €k	Year 5 €k
Profit after tax	135	142	150	159	170
Increase in operating assets	55	66	77	89	10
Free cash flow	80	76	72	71	160

chapter, shareholders prefer to receive a given amount of cash sooner rather than later, and they prefer the business to take fewer risks in the process of generating that cash. It follows that, other things being equal, a business that can generate cash for its shareholders sooner and with lower risk will have a higher valuation. We will now explore how this works.

The value of expected future cash flows

The process of valuation is best explained by means of a simple example. Take a look at the first three rows in Table 8.5, which report cash flows over a period of three years for investments A, B and C. In each case, there is a cash outflow of €100 on the first day of the first year ('year 0'), followed by cash inflows on the last day of the first year ('year 1') for A, the second year for B and the third year for C.

As we will see, a given amount of money received at a future date has a lower value than the same amount received at the present date: you would rather have €100 now than €100 two years from now. We refer to the value of money at the present date as 'present value'. In Table 8.5, the investment of €100 at the first day of the first year has a present value of €100. Each of the future cash inflows has a present value also, but for the moment all we can say is that this amount is somewhat lower than its face value. The process of valuation is to convert all expected future cash flows into present values: we want to know what all of these future cash flows are worth to us now.

The cash inflows in Table 8.5 are in each case returns on an investment of €100. In general, the average, annual rate of return earned over the lifetime of an investment is called the internal rate of return (IRR). For investment A, the IRR is 10 per cent, because an investment of €100 is made at the start of the year and €110 has been earned by the end of the year. The IRR for investment B is also 10 per cent. While the cash inflow is greater in this case, so too is the time over which it is earned: an amount of €100, invested

Table 8.5 Valuation of cash flows

		Year 0 €	Year 1 €	Year 2 €	Year 3 €
Cash flows	Investment A	−100	110	0	0
	Investment B	−100	0	121	0
	Investment C	−100	0	0	133
Compound 10% return		1.00	1.10	1.21	1.33
Discount factor (1/compound return)		1.00	0.91	0.83	0.75
Present value of cash flow	Investment A	−100	100	0	0
	Investment B	−100	0	100	0
	Investment C	−100	0	0	100

over two years at a compound return of 10 per cent, becomes worth €121. Following the same reasoning, the IRR for investment C is also 10 per cent.

The IRR is similar to the return on equity (ROE) and return on capital employed (ROCE) in that it measures the rate of return on an investment. An important difference is that the ROE and ROCE are measures for a single period of time, while the IRR is a forward-looking measure that captures all of the expected cash flows over the lifetime of an investment. The IRR is used prospectively, when making an investment decision, while the ROE and ROCE are typically used retrospectively, in measuring the actual return earned in each year by past investments.

We saw in Chapter 6 that the ROE, or the ROCE, can be compared with the cost of capital in order to measure economic profit; if the return earned by a business exceeds its cost of capital, then economic profit is positive and value is created. Following the same reasoning, the IRR can also be compared with the cost of capital; if the IRR on an investment project exceeds the cost of capital for the project, then value is created, meaning that investors become better off than they would otherwise have been had they invested their money elsewhere.

What we will now see is that we can measure exactly how much value an investment is expected to generate. By using what is termed a discounted cash flow (DCF) model, we can express all expected future cash flows in terms of their present values. We can then compare these present values with the cost of making the investment, to determine an estimate of value-creation termed net present value (NPV). Just as economic profit measures value creation for a single period of time, so NPV captures value creation for an investment as a whole. Equally, just as an excess of profit over the cost of capital leads to positive economic profit, so too an IRR higher than the cost of capital leads to a positive NPV. We can see how all of this works by taking another look at the investments in Table 8.5.

We have seen that all three of the investments in Table 8.5 generate the same IRR, meaning that they have the same compounded annual return. For example, in the case of investment A, the cash flow is 110 per cent of the initial investment, and for investment B, it is 121 per cent; these compound returns are reported in the fourth row of Table 8.5. An alternative way to think about these numbers is in terms of discounting, which is the opposite of compounding. So, taking the example of investment B, instead of thinking in terms of €121 being a 10 per cent compound return on €100, we can reverse this and instead think of €100 as being €121 discounted over two years at an annual rate of 10 per cent. Likewise, €110 discounted at 10 per cent over one year is equal to €100. The rate at which a future cash flow is discounted to equate it to its present value is called a discount rate, which in this case is 10 per cent. The ratio of a present value to its cash flow counterpart in any given future year is called a discount factor, which is equal simply to one over the relevant compound rate of return. This is all shown in the fifth row of Table 8.5. These concepts sound more complicated than they really are, and so it is worth spending a little time reviewing Table 8.5 and making sure that you understand how each of the numbers is determined and how they relate to compounding and discounting.

At first sight, the purpose of discounting is not intuitive, and to make it so it will be helpful to return to our central purpose in this chapter, which is to value future cash flows. In Table 8.5, we started with a present value and a future cash flow, and we worked out the implicit rate of return (the IRR). If you think back to Table 8.4, however, the problem is set out rather differently. What we have is an estimate of future cash flows, and what we want to know is their present value. So, we are necessarily discounting rather than compounding. What we need is an appropriate mechanism for discounting future cash flows so that we know what they are currently worth. This is the process of valuation.

To illustrate, suppose that you are invited to make an investment, which will cost you €100 in cash today, and from which you will receive €110 in cash one year from now. Should you make the investment, and why?

One way to answer this question is to reason as follows. The €100 that you have today could either be committed to this investment, or else it could be invested elsewhere. If the return that you could achieve elsewhere exceeds 10 per cent, then you will have more than €110 in one year's time, and so you would be better off with this alternative investment. If you cannot achieve 10 per cent elsewhere, however, then making the investment and receiving the €110 would be the better decision. What you are doing here is comparing the IRR on the investment (i.e. 10 per cent) with the cost of capital (i.e. your opportunity cost, or the return that you could achieve by investing elsewhere). The decision rule is that if the IRR exceeds the cost of capital, then you should invest.

Now suppose that the question is expressed somewhat differently. Suppose that you are asked how much cash you would pay today for the right to receive €110 in cash one year from now, and suppose that your cost of capital is 6 per cent. You are being asked to determine the present value of the €110: what is it worth to you, today, to have the right to receive €110 one year from now? This is the question that we are asking when valuing a business. We can estimate the cash flows that the business will generate in the future, as we have done in Table 8.4, and our question is what these cash flows are worth now.

The number we are looking for is the amount which, if invested today at a return of 6 per cent, would be worth €110 one year from now. The logic behind this calculation is that it takes into account your opportunity cost. As an investment of €1 today would be worth €1.06 if the return is 6 per cent, then an investment of €103.77 (which is €110/1.06) would be worth €110. So, if €103.77 is required in an alternative investment in order to return €110, then if you pay more than this amount for the current investment, you would be over-paying. This is because the higher initial cost of the investment makes your expected return lower than 6 per cent. Similarly, if you pay less than €103.77 for the investment, then your return would be higher than 6 per cent. In other words, your IRR on the investment would exceed your cost of capital, and the investment would be value-creating for you. In short, what your calculation is doing is setting a value on the investment that makes it no more or less attractive to you than the alternative investment that you could make: you would either create or lose value by paying an amount different from €103.77, which makes €103.77 the amount that the investment is worth to you.

The general principle is that the discount rate for expected future cash flows should be the cost of capital. This is illustrated in the final rows in Table 8.5, where the present values of the future cash flows have been calculated, in each case by multiplying the cash flow by its respective discount factor. You will see that, for each of the three investments, the present value of the future cash flow is €100, which is equal to the cost of the investment, meaning that there is zero NPV. This should not be surprising because, in each case the IRR and the cost of capital are the same, meaning that, in this particular example, value is neither created nor destroyed.

If, for the sake of argument, the cash inflows had been higher in Table 8.5 while the initial investment had remained the same, then the IRR would have been higher and the present value of the cash inflows would have exceeded the initial investment, giving positive NPV. If, on the other hand, the cash flows and the IRR remained unchanged but the cost of capital was higher, then NPV would have been negative. In general, the cost of capital increases with the perceived riskiness of the investment such that, other things being equal, riskier expected cash flows will have a lower present value. The appropriate cost of capital to use in any present value calculation is for an alternative investment of equivalent risk.

We are now in a position to complete our valuation, which is done in Table 8.6. You should look first at the data in each of the five years in our forecast (there is also a column for 'terminal value' which we will return to shortly). In each year, there an estimated free cash flow, a discount factor (assuming a 10 per cent cost of capital) and a present value. So, for example, the free cash flow of €160k generated in year 5 has a present value of €99k, because an investment of €99k made at the present time at a rate of return of 10 per cent would become worth €160k by the end of five years.

The only component of our valuation that remains to be discussed is the terminal value. We have estimated the free cash flow for the forthcoming five years, but we have not yet considered what will happen in years 6 and beyond. We could, of course, make individual forecasts for years 6, 7, 8 and so on, but we face the reality that forecasting too far into the future is too unreliable to be worthwhile, and it is for this reason that we extended our forecast for only five years. While forecasting may not be reliable, however, we do still have a business at the end of year 5, and this business clearly has a

Table 8.6 Corporate valuation

		Year 1 €k	Year 2 €k	Year 3 €k	Year 4 €k	Year 5 €k	Terminal value €k
Profit after tax		135	142	150	159	170	1,700
Increase in operating assets		55	66	77	89	10	
Free cash flow		80	76	72	71	160	
Discount factor		0.91	0.83	0.75	0.68	0.62	0.62
Present value		72	62	54	48	99	1,056
Business value	1,393						

value at that date. In order for our business valuation to be complete, therefore, we need to not only value the free cash flows for the next five years but also to put a value on the business as it stands at the end of five years, and it is this amount which is called the terminal value.

In practice, and because we lack more reliable methods for seeing into the future, the terminal value is typically calculated in a very simple way. The most common assumption is that the business as it exists at the end of year 5 will continue to exist indefinitely, with the same level of assets and the same annual profit. There will be no difference between profit and free cash flow in such a situation, because cash is by assumption not reinvested to grow operating assets. In Table 8.6, there is an annual profit/cash of €170k that we assume will continue to be generated indefinitely. This annual profit stream is equivalent to a capital value of €1,700k. To see this, imagine that you have €1,700k in the bank and that it earns 10 per cent in interest each year. One year from now, if you spend your interest income of €170k, you will still have €1,700k in the bank, and again two years from now, and three years, and so on. In other words, at a rate of return of 10 per cent a capital value of €1,700k will generate an indefinite income stream of €170k each year; alternatively stated, annual profit/cash of €170k has a value of €1,700k at the end of year 5.

Once this amount is discounted, it has a present value of €1,056k: at a cost of capital of 10 per cent, a current investment of €1,056k would grow to €1,700k after 5 years, which is the estimated value of the business at that time.

Our estimate of the total present value of the business is €1,393, which is simply the sum of present value of the free cash flows from each of the five years in our forecast, plus the terminal value.

In summary

This chapter has illustrated a forward-looking role for financial statement information. In particular, by means of working through a simple set of financial statements, we have demonstrated the fundamental components of a business valuation.

There are, in essence, two stages in the process of valuation. First there is the forecasting of cash flows, and we have seen how this can be done by means of forecasting the income statement and the balance sheet. Second, there is the discounting of these cash flows to their present values, which are aggregated to give an overall valuation.

In practice, the valuation of a business is more complex, of course, and it would include dealing with issues that we have not addressed in this chapter, such as the depreciation of PPE, interest expenses and debt financing and so on. What we have done, however, is cover the fundamentals. Any business valuation that you come across will be grounded in the framework and analysis that we have covered in this chapter.

Appendix 1

The lexicon of accounting can seem extensive and confusing, and so it is helpful to have a concise summary. This is the spirit in which this glossary has been compiled. The definitions provided here are not technical and impenetrable, but instead informal and explanatory. So, for example, while several of the definitions are similar to those in international accounting standards, they differ wherever a more relaxed use of language helps to convey meaning.

Accounting The process of identifying, measuring and communicating economic information, with the purpose of informing decision making relating to the financial performance and financial position of an organisation.

Accounting policies The specific principles, bases, conventions, rules and practices applied by an entity in preparing and presenting financial statements.

Accounts payable, or creditors A liability comprising amounts for which an invoice has been received but cash settlement remains outstanding, for example arising as a result of purchases made on credit.

Accounts receivable, or debtors An asset comprising amounts that have been invoiced but cash has yet to be received, typically arising as a result of sales made on credit.

Accounts receivable turnover A ratio measuring the time taken to collect cash from customers. Accounts receivable result from revenue that has been recognised but not yet received in cash, and so a comparison of the outstanding accounts receivable balance at the end of a reporting period with the total revenue recognised during that period indicates how quickly revenue is converted into cash. Specifically, accounts receivable turnover is defined as (accounts receivable/annual revenue) × 365 days.

Accrual basis of accounting The effects of transactions and other events are recognised when they occur (and not as cash or its equivalent is received or paid) and they are recorded in the accounting records and reported in the financial statements of the periods to which they relate.

Amortisation The systematic allocation of the depreciable amount of an asset over its useful life. In effect, amortisation is an alternative term for depreciation. It is typically applied to intangible assets, while depreciation is applied to tangible assets.

Asset A resource controlled by the entity as a result of past events and from which future economic benefits are expected to flow to the entity.

Associate An entity, including an unincorporated entity such as a partnership, over which the investor has significant influence and that is neither a subsidiary nor an interest in a joint venture.

Balance sheet Financial statement that presents the relationship of an entity's assets, liabilities and equity at a point in time.

Book value The amount at which a given item is recorded in the balance sheet. An asset may have an actual, economic value that exceeds its book value, although the opposite should not, in principle, be the case. For example, the book value of land and buildings may be the amount that was originally paid on acquisition (historical cost), while the amount that could be realised on disposal (economic value) might be significantly greater. If, however, the economic value declines to an amount below the book value, then the latter should be written down, so that book value and economic value are equal.

Breakeven The level of output at which total income is equal to total expenses.

Budget A set of financial projections, typically for income and expenses, but also for capital expenditure and cash flow, which is, first, a financial representation of planned business activity and, second, a benchmark against which to control and evaluate realised business performance.

Business combination The bringing together of separate entities or businesses into one reporting entity.

Capital employed The total investment made by shareholders and debt holders of an organisation – i.e. the total value of equity plus debt.

Capitalise Expenditure is said to be capitalised, as opposed to expensed, when it leads to the creation of a new asset on the balance sheet. Hence, it is typical for a cash outflow classified as investing to be capitalised, while an operating cash outflow is expensed.

Carrying amount The amount at which an asset or liability is recognised in the balance sheet.

Cash flows Inflows and outflows of cash.

Cash flow statement Financial statement that provides information about the changes in cash of an entity for a period, showing separately changes during the period from operating, investing and financing activities.

Class of assets A grouping of assets of a similar nature and use in an entity's operations.

Component of an entity Operations and cash flows that can be clearly distinguished, operationally and for financial reporting purposes, from the rest of the entity.

Consolidated financial statements The financial statements of a group of entities consisting of a parent and one or more subsidiaries.

Contingent liability (a) A possible obligation that arises from past events and whose existence will be confirmed only by the occurrence or non-occurrence of one or more uncertain future events not wholly within the control of the entity; or (b) a present obligation that arises from past events but is not recognised because: (i) it is not probable that an outflow of resources embodying economic benefits will be required to settle the obligation; or (ii) the amount of the obligation cannot be measured with sufficient reliability.

Control (of an entity) The power to govern the financial and operating policies of an entity so as to obtain benefits from its activities.

Contribution The incremental effect on profit from a transaction with customers, equal to sales revenue less variable cost of making the sale.

Cost of capital The percentage return on capital that providers of finance expect to earn; also known as the cost of equity when applied to shareholders' funds, or the rate of interest when applied to the cost of debt finance. If a company is funded by both equity and debt finance, then its overall cost of capital is an average of the cost of equity and the interest rate, weighted by the proportions of equity and debt in the capital structure; this is known as the weighted average cost of capital, or WACC.

Cost of goods sold Expenses that are directly attributable to units of output, notably materials and other components of inventory.

Credit See double-entry accounting.

Creditors See accounts payable.

Current asset An asset that is expected to be converted into cash within one year, notably inventory, accounts receivable and cash.

Current liability A liability that is expected to be settled by cash payment within one year, notably accounts payable (to suppliers, tax authorities and so on) and short-term financing obligations.

Current ratio A measure of liquidity, equal to the ratio value of current assets to current liabilities.

Debit See double-entry accounting.

Debt A liability, representing finance provided to an organisation at a contractually agreed rate of interest. Debt and equity together comprise the capital employed by a company.

Debtors See accounts receivable.

Depreciable amount The cost of an asset less its residual value.

Depreciation The systematic allocation of the depreciable amount of an asset over its useful life. In effect, depreciation is an alternative term for amortisation. It is typically applied to tangible assets, while amortisation is applied to intangible assets.

Discontinued operation A component of an entity that either has been disposed of, or is classified as held for sale, and (a) represents a separate major line of business or geographical area of operations; (b) is part of a single coordinated plan to dispose of a separate major line of business or geographical area of operations; or (c) is a subsidiary acquired exclusively with a view to resale.

Discounting A method of converting cash flows expected to take place at various future dates into their equivalent present values.

Direct cost A cost that varies in direct proportion with output: any increase in output results in an extra direct cost.

Dividend A payment made by a company to its shareholders, as a distribution of profit earned by the company.

Dividend yield Defined as dividends per share divided by the share price, the dividend yield is a simple measure of the cash withdrawn from a company by shareholders as a percentage of the value of their investment. The sum of the dividend yield and the percentage increase in the share price (i.e. the percentage capital gain, excluding the amount paid out as dividend) measures the total return to shareholders during a period of time.

Double-entry accounting The underlying mechanism of record-keeping in accounting, whereby every transaction or event is recorded in the form of a journal entry, comprising a debit to one individual account and an equal credit to another. A debit entry is an increase in an asset, or a decrease in equity or in a liability. A credit entry is the opposite of a debit entry, such that the effect of a journal entry, in simultaneously debiting one account and crediting another, is to ensure that a balance sheet always remains balanced. The collective term for all individual accounts is the general ledger, and balances are drawn from the general ledger in order to present summary information in the financial statements.

EBIT, or operating profit Earnings before interest and tax; a measure of profit earned by an organisation's operating activities.

EBITDA Earnings before interest, tax, depreciation and amortisation; a measure of performance that is something of a hybrid between operating profit and operating cash flow, being based upon EBIT but excluding depreciation and amortisation, which are typically the largest accruals (non-cash items).

Economic profit A measure of profit that includes a notional cost for the use of shareholders' funds, sometimes referred to as economic value added, or residual income. A positive economic profit implies that the company is achieving a better return on shareholders' funds than could be achieved if those funds were invested elsewhere. Economic profit is therefore a measure of shareholder value creation.

Enterprise value The total economic value of a company, defined as the sum of shareholder value (market capitalisation) and the market value of debt, which equals the economic value of the company's net assets.

eps (earnings per share) Profit after tax/number of shares in issue; used primarily in the PE ratio.

Equity The residual interest in the assets of the entity after deducting all its liabilities.

Expenses Decreases in economic benefits during the reporting period in the form of outflows or depletions of assets or incurrences of liabilities that result in decreases in equity, other than those relating to distributions to equity participants.

Fair value The amount for which an asset could be exchanged or a liability settled between knowledgeable, willing parties in an arm's length transaction.

Financial accounting The external reporting of the financial statements and related information, primarily for the purpose of the organisation's providers of finance.

Financial asset Any asset that is: (a) cash; (b) an equity instrument of another entity; (c) a contractual right to receive cash or another financial asset.

Financial instrument A contract that gives rise to a financial asset of one entity and a financial liability or equity instrument of another entity.

Financial liability Any liability that is a contractual obligation to deliver cash or another financial asset to another entity.

Financial position The relationship of the assets, liabilities and equity of an entity as reported in the balance sheet.

Financial statements Structured representation of the financial position, financial performance and cash flows of an entity.

Financing activities Activities that result in changes in the size and composition of the contributed equity and borrowings of the entity, reported as a category in the cash flow statement.

Fixed assets Assets held for ongoing use within the business, with an expected life exceeding one year.

Fixed costs Costs that do not vary with output during a specified period of time.

GAAP Generally accepted accounting practice – i.e. the set of rules and regulations that make up accounting standards for external financial reporting.

Gains Increases in economic benefits that meet the definition of income but that are not revenue.

Gearing See leverage.

General ledger See double-entry accounting.

Going concern An entity is a going concern unless management either intends to liquidate the entity or to cease trading, or has no realistic alternative but to do so.

Goodwill Future economic benefits arising from assets that are not capable of being individually identified and separately recognised.

Gross profit A subtotal in the income statement, equal to revenue less cost of goods sold, typically expressed as a percentage gross profit margin.

IRR (internal rate of return) The average economic rate of return earned over the life of an investment. If the IRR is equal to the cost of capital, then the investment has a net present value of zero, because the amount that is earned is equal to the return expected by investors. If the IRR exceeds the cost of capital, then value is created.

Indirect cost A cost that does not vary in direct proportion with output.

Impairment loss, or write-down The amount by which the carrying amount of an asset exceeds its economic value.

Income Increases in economic benefits during the reporting period in the form of inflows or enhancements of assets or decreases of liabilities that result in increases in equity, other than those relating to contributions from equity participants.

Income statement Financial statement that presents information about the performance of an entity for a period, i.e. the relationship of its income and expenses.

Intangible asset An identifiable non-monetary asset without physical substance. Such an asset is identifiable when it: (a) is separable, i.e. is capable of being separated or divided from the entity and sold, transferred, licensed, rented or exchanged, either individually or together with a related contract, asset or liability; or (b) arises from contractual or other legal rights, regardless of whether those rights are transferable or separable from the entity or from other rights and obligations.

Interim financial report A financial report containing either a complete set of financial statements or a set of condensed financial statements for an interim period (i.e. a financial reporting period shorter than a full financial year).

International Financial Reporting Standards (IFRSs) Standards and Interpretations adopted by the International Accounting Standards Board (IASB).

Inventory, or stock An asset: (a) held for sale in the ordinary course of business; (b) in the process of production for such sale; or (c) in the form of materials or supplies to be consumed in the production process or in the rendering of services.

Inventory turnover A ratio measuring the holding period for inventory, defined as (inventory/annual cost of sales) $\times$ 365 days.

Investing activities The acquisition and disposal of long-term assets and other investments, reported as a category in the cash flow statement.

Investment property Property (land or a building, or part of a building, or both) held (by the owner or by the lessee under a finance lease) to earn rentals or for capital appreciation or both, rather than for: (a) use in the production or supply of goods or services or for administrative purposes; or (b) sale in the ordinary course of business.

Journal entry See double-entry accounting.

Leverage, or gearing (financial) The relationship between debt and equity in a company's capital structure, defined as debt/capital employed. High financial leverage implies relatively high variation in ROE resulting from variation in ROCE.

Leverage, or gearing (operating) The relationship between variable costs and fixed costs, defined as fixed costs/total costs. High operating leverage implies relatively high variation in profit resulting from variation in output.

Liability A present obligation of the entity arising from past events, the settlement of which is expected to result in an outflow from the entity of resources embodying economic benefits.

Liquidity Nearness to cash. An asset or liability is said to be more liquid if it can be more readily converted into cash, meaning converted more quickly and at relatively little risk of change in value.

Loans payable Financial liabilities other than short-term trade payables on normal credit terms.

Management accounting The reporting of the financial statements and related information within an organisation, for the purposes of decision making by management.

Market capitalisation, or shareholder value The value on the stock market of the publicly traded equity of a company, defined as share price × number of shares.

Material Omissions or misstatements of items are material if they could, individually or collectively, influence the economic decisions of users taken on the basis of the financial statements. Materiality depends on the size and nature of the omission or misstatement judged in the surrounding circumstances. The size or nature of the item, or a combination of both, could be the determining factor.

Measurement The process of determining the monetary amounts at which the elements of the financial statements are to be recognised and carried in the balance sheet and income statement.

Net assets The total value of assets less liabilities. Net assets in the balance sheet must be equal to equity. If the value of net assets changes, then this is either because the organisation has: (a) made a profit or loss; or (b) received an additional investment from its shareholders or transferred funds to its shareholders.

Net operating profit after tax (NOPAT) Defined as operating profit × (1 − tax rate).

Net present value (NPV) Defined as the present value generated by an investment, less the cost of making that investment. An investment that has a positive net present value is by definition value-creating, meaning that it provides a better investment opportunity than would be otherwise available to investors.

Notes (to financial statements) Notes contain information in addition to that presented in the balance sheet, income statement, statement of changes in equity and cash flow statement. Notes provide narrative descriptions or disaggregations of items disclosed in those statements and information about items that do not qualify for recognition in those statements.

Objective of financial statements To provide information about the financial position, performance and cash flows of an entity that is useful for economic decision-making by a broad range of users who are not in a position to demand reports tailored to meet their particular information needs.

Operating activities The principal revenue-producing activities of the entity and other activities that are not investing or financing activities, reported as a category in the cash flow statement.

Operating profit See EBIT.

Operating segment An operating segment is a component of an entity: (a) that engages in business activities from which it may earn revenues and incur expenses (including revenues and expenses relating to transactions with other components of the same entity); (b) whose operating results are regularly reviewed by the entity's chief operating decision maker to make decisions about resources to be allocated to the segment and assess its performance; and (c) for which discrete financial information is available.

Opportunity cost The value foregone by choosing one course of action over another. If, for example, a given sum of money is used to purchase shares in a company, then it cannot be invested elsewhere, and the value foregone by not being able to invest elsewhere is the cost of not taking that opportunity. If the actual return exceeds the opportunity cost, then value is created.

Overhead Costs that are indirect, meaning that they do not vary in direct proportion with output. Such costs may be independent of variation in output, in which case they are fixed, or they may be related, in which case they are termed variable overheads.

PE ratio A valuation measure used by investors, typically when comparing one company with another, defined as the ratio of share price to earnings per share (share price/eps). If a company has a high PE ratio, then either: (a) it is expected to have high earnings growth; (b) it is perceived to be a low-risk investment; or (c) it is overpriced by stock market investors.

Performance The relationship of the income and expenses of an entity, as reported in the income statement.

Present value A current estimate of the present discounted value of future net cash flows.

Profit The residual amount that remains after expenses have been deducted from income.

Profit and loss account (P&L) See income statement.

Profit margin Profit expressed as a percentage of sales, typically either as a gross profit margin (gross profit/sales), operating profit margin (operating profit/sales) or net profit margin (profit after tax/sales).

Property, plant and equipment (PPE) Tangible assets that: (a) are held for use in the production or supply of goods or services, for rental to others, for investment or for administrative purposes and (b) are expected to be used during more than one period.

Provision A liability of uncertain timing or amount.

Prudence The inclusion of a degree of caution in the exercise of the judgements needed in making the estimates required under conditions of uncertainty, such that assets or income are not overstated and liabilities or expenses are not understated.

Realisation The process of conversion into cash. For example, when an asset such as a building or a holding of shares is sold, the value is said to be realised. If the value of asset has increased while in the possession of an organisation, but the asset remains on the balance sheet and has not yet been sold, then there is said to be an unrealised gain.

Recognition The process of incorporating in the balance sheet or income statement an item that satisfies the following criteria: (a) it is probable that any future economic benefit associated with the item will flow to or from the entity; and (b) the item has a cost or value that can be measured with reliability.

Relevance The quality of information that allows it to influence the economic decisions of users by helping them evaluate past, present or future events or confirming, or correcting, their past evaluations.

Reliability The quality of information that makes it free from material error and bias and represent faithfully that which it either purports to represent or could reasonably be expected to represent.

Reporting date The end of the latest period covered by financial statements or by an interim financial report.

Reporting period The period covered by financial statements, which for external financial reporting purposes is typically a quarter, half or full year.

Residual value (of an asset) The estimated amount that an entity would currently obtain from disposal of an asset, after deducting the estimated costs of disposal, if the asset were already of the age and in the condition expected at the end of its useful life.

Retained profit A component of equity, equal to the cumulative profit earned by a company less the cumulative dividends paid to shareholders; it is the amount of profit that has been earned and retained.

Return on capital employed (ROCE) Defined as either operating profit/capital employed or as NOPAT/capital employed; a measure of the rate of return on the total equity and debt investment in the company.

Return on equity (ROE) Defined as profit after tax/equity; a measure of the rate of return on shareholders' investment in the company.

Revenue The gross inflow of economic benefits during the period arising in the course of the ordinary activities of an entity when those inflows result in increases in equity, other than increases relating to contributions from equity participants.

Share, or stock An equity investment. A shareholder invests cash in a company in exchange for a percentage ownership (a share) of the equity of that company. Ownership of shares can be traded on a stock market.

Shareholder value See market capitalisation.

Statement of changes in equity Financial statement that presents the profit or loss for a period, items of income and expense recognised directly in equity for the period, the effects of changes in accounting policy and corrections of errors recognised in the period, and (depending on the format of the statement of changes in equity chosen by the entity) the amounts of transactions with equity holders acting in their capacity as equity holders during the period.

Stock See Inventory or Share.

Tax expense (tax income) The aggregate amount included in the determination of profit or loss for the period in respect of current tax and deferred tax.

Taxable profit (tax loss) The profit (loss) for a period, determined in accordance with the rules established by the taxation authorities, upon which income taxes are payable (recoverable)

Timeliness Providing the information in financial statements within the decision time frame.

Total shareholder return (TSR) The sum of the dividend yield and the percentage increase in the share price (i.e. the percentage capital gain, excluding the amount paid out as dividend).

Understandability The quality of information that makes it comprehensible by users who have a reasonable knowledge of business and economic activities and accounting and a willingness to study the information with reasonable diligence.

Useful life The period over which an asset is expected to be available for use by an entity or the number of production or similar units expected to be obtained from the asset by an entity.

Variable costs Costs that vary with output. Variable costs can be direct, if they vary in direct proportion with output, or they can be indirect (variable overheads), in which case the relationship with output is less straightforward.

WACC See cost of capital.

Working capital Defined as current assets less current liabilities (i.e. current net assets), working capital is a measure of the amount of finance needed to fund an organisation's operating cycle – i.e. it is the investment required for a given level of (in particular) inventory and accounts receivable, offset by the amount of accounts payable. Cash, bank overdrafts and other financing items can be excluded from working capital, on the basis that they relate to the financing of the organisation, as opposed to being an investment in its operations.

Write-down See impairment loss.

Appendix 2

Further reading

There are many books and other sources on accounting, and so if you would like to extend your knowledge beyond the introductory material in this book, then you have no shortage of options. The following illustrates some of the sources that you might consider.

The following three books all support general accounting courses, such as those at MBA level. While each is longer and more comprehensive than this book, you should find progression to the material in these books fairly comfortable.

Stolowy, H., Lebas, M. and Ding, Y. (2010). *Financial Accounting and Reporting: A Global Perspective*, Cengage Learning (3rd edn).

Walton, P. and Aerts, W. (2009). *Global Financial Accounting and Reporting*, Cengage Learning (2nd edn).

Weetman, P. (2006). *Financial and Management Accounting, An Introduction*, Pearson (4th edn).

The following books are more advanced. They are good sources for those wishing to explore more fully the analysis of financial statements and the links between accounting information and corporate valuation.

Healy, P. and Palepu, K. (2007). *Business Analysis and Valuation: Using Financial Statements*. Thomson Southwestern (4th edn).

Penman, S.H. (2009). *Financial Statement Analysis and Security Valuation*, McGraw-Hill (4th edn).

As a complement to the study of accounting, a knowledge of finance is helpful. The following are both standard references in this field.

Brealey, R., Myers, S., and Allen, F. (2011). *Principles of Corporate Finance*, McGraw-Hill (10th edn).

Koller, T., Goedhart M., and Wessels D. (2010). *Valuation: Measuring and Managing the Value of Companies*, Wiley (5th edn).

If you are interested in topical information about specific rules and regulations regarding financial reporting, then there are two particularly informative online sources to consider. The first is the accounting standard-setters themselves, notably the International Accounting Standards Board (IASB – www.iasb. org) and, for the USA, the Financial Accounting Standards Board (FASB – www.fasb.org). The second is the websites of the Big Four accounting firms (Deloitte – deloitte.com; Ernst & Young – ey.com; KPMG – kpmg.com; and PriceWaterhouseCoopers – pwc.com), which have a wealth of downloadable information.

Index